# Supper Time

# Supper Time

## LEON HALE

WINEDALE PUBLISHING
Houston

Published by Winedale Publishing Co., Houston
Distributed by the Texas A&M University Press Consortium

Illustrations © by Barbara Mathews Whitehead

Library of Congress Cataloguing-in-Publication Data
Hale, Leon.
Supper Time / Leon Hale.
p.   cm.
ISBN   0-965-7468-3-6
1. Cookery
Biography.   I. Title
TX 651.H29      1999
641.5—dc21              99-40019

Winedale website address: www.tamu.edu/upress/wp

Manufactured in the United States of America
2 4 6 8 9 7 5 3

*Book Design by Harriet Correll*

To the memory of Bill Shearer

# Acknowledgments

I would like to thank the following persons for providing recipes and recollections that enabled me to write *Supper Time* and call it my book: My two sisters, Maifred Hale Cullen and Ima Ruth Hale Taylor; my daughter Rebecca Hale Fisher; Shirley and Buck Sloan; Marie Moore; Koleen Vick; Emmie Lou Green; Jim and Phyllis Miniatis; Opal Pearson; Glenn Whitehead; Rusty Mitchum; Old Friend (C.E.) Morgan; and Vicente and Rosario Borrego.

Special thanks also to the editor of this book, Babette Fraser, who caused my pronouns to agree with their antecedents and fixed all the recipes in proper form, in case anybody wants to try them.

# Contents

# Supper Time

# Author's Note

In rural Texas where I originated, the evening meal was always called supper, never dinner. Dinner was at noon. Lunch was what you ate in the middle of the day but you ate it away from home, at school or at work or on a picnic. We might "go home for lunch," as we said, but when we got there what we ate was dinner.

Early in 1943, when I was in the Army and stationed at Scott Field, Illinois, one Saturday night I met a friendly girl in a St. Louis night club called Tune Town. We danced and talked and got along all right and she invited me to come eat Sunday dinner at her apartment. This was the best offer I'd had since I left civilian life so the next day I slicked myself up and took a street car according to her directions and knocked on that young lady's door at 11:30 A.M.

There was no answer for a full minute. I rapped again, and at last the door opened about an inch and through that crack I could see one sleepy brown eye, part of an ear and a couple of hairpins. Nothing more.

She said, "Come back at seven o'clock."

I pulled that social boner more than half a century ago, but even now when somebody mentions dinner to me, I need to remind myself that they're talking about the evening meal.

Many Americans of rural beginnings still call their evening meal supper. The usage is fading, though. Most dictionaries now say that supper is an evening meal, all right, but a light one, served when a substantial meal is eaten in the middle of the day. In this book, which is sort of old-fashioned, when a meal is called supper, whether it's heavy or not, it's eaten at night.

Mainly what you'll find on the pages that follow is the tale of one man's love affair with the food that has sustained him for more than three-quarters of a century. Food like black-eyed peas, pinto beans, pork chops, turnips and greens, cornbread and butter, chicken and dumplings, bacon and eggs and biscuits, steaks cooked in the back yard, stews of half a dozen kinds, chili con carne—known to me as chili—and a long menu of other Mexican-style dishes.

Also I'll record a few of what I call my food adventures, from a time when I was trying to cook for myself. Some of those now seem truly outrageous and I'm not sure I'd care to experience them again, although they are fun to remember. I also want to explore the mysterious eating habits of men, especially when their women are not around. And their compulsion to sneak away now and then and cook for themselves in the woods and on river banks.

Most of the meals I'm recalling here would not pass the health-food test. They're loaded with saturated fat. But this is not a health book. It's not a cookbook, either, though it includes a few of my favorite recipes. Toward the end we'll deal with some favorable substitutes for the fat-laden comfort foods I grew up on. But those old-fashioned dishes will always be my favorites, and I'll never stop wanting them.

Supper Time, as much as anything else, is my way of saying goodbye to the food I loved so well, because there's not much of it I can eat any longer.

# The Apartment

*I*n January of 1981, when I was sixty years old, I began what I then thought would be the greatest adventure of my life, and I was almost right.

The adventure was bachelorhood, and living alone. Other than during the year or so after I got out of the Army in 1945, I had never lived in a place that didn't have a resident woman who cooked and washed clothes and kept house and doctored people who got sick in the middle of the night. And spent more of my money than I did.

In the beginning of the adventure I was a long way from flush. In fact I was fresh out of divorce court and my plow had been cleaned. My most valuable possession was a crippled station wagon that wasn't worth what I owed on it. That's what I ended up with after thirty years of working, sometimes at three different jobs all at once.

But I had held onto my newspaper column and I moved into this three-room apartment in Houston, to start all over. Most of my contemporaries in the work force were talking about retiring then. A few had already quit at fifty-five.

That apartment had a nice refrigerator and a four-burner electric stove. The first few weeks I kept the fridge full of beer, and used the stove to heat water for instant coffee and that's about all. I'd never done any cooking, other than frying a few eggs and burning steaks on a back yard barbecue barrel. But I wasn't worried about food. A dozen restaurants were within walking distance of that apartment.

After six weeks I was sick of eating in every one of them, and started bringing home lunch meat and bread and mayonnaise and sometimes even a head of iceberg lettuce and a tomato, for sandwiches. It hadn't yet hit me that I needed to start cooking. I didn't have anything to cook in, anyway. I didn't even have a skillet, or a stew pot.

Well, I did have one pot. My friend Osa Lee Jones ran the Seagull Restaurant at San Leon until he got sick and died and his widow Georgia closed the business. In appreciation of all the nights I'd sat in that place, increasing revenues, Georgia gave me a four-gallon cook pot out of the restaurant's kitchen. Osa Lee used it to cook beans for his customers. A pot that size didn't seem appropriate in a bachelor apartment occupied by one bachelor but I liked having the pot, and displayed it as a decoration. Later it would become very useful to me.

I also had a beautiful red Texas star quilt made by Annie Schaate of Round Top. It was far too nice to use as a bed cover so I hung it on my wall and it was the only piece of art I had in that place for several months. Some days when I was feeling low I would sit on the carpet and face that pretty quilt and its intricate patterns would seem to move, in and out, as if it were breathing, and somehow this was a comfort to me.

For fifty bucks I bought a second-hand single bed with box springs and for seventy-five more I acquired a black sofa from Jorjanna Price, a *Houston Post* reporter who was moving to Austin to join the paper's bureau there. About this same time my friend David Fowler lost his radio talk show job at KPRC. He and his bride decided to sell everything they owned that wouldn't fit in their car and leave town, and just go somewhere else and see what happened. That notion appealed to me and I wanted to go with them and I might have, except I still had the regular pay coming in for doing the column. Newspapers all over the country were folding then, and no reasonably sober journalist walked away from a job.

Just before the Fowlers drove off to seek a new fortune they sold me their TV, on credit, for a hundred and fifty bucks. And they threw in a nice brass spittoon and that touched me, because I'd always wanted a brass spittoon.

So, that's how I was equipped to start my new life. A four-gallon bean pot, a second-hand bed, a quilt on the wall, a black sofa, a used TV, a worn-out station wagon and a brass spittoon.

The first thing that happened to me, I came down with a severe case of insomnia. I slept so little I could have done without the bed and saved fifty bucks. I couldn't stand to stay in that apartment all the time so I did a lot of roaming in the middle of the night. I began going into twenty-four-hour supermarkets because, at first, theirs were the only well lighted and friendly doors open to the public at 3 A.M.

All-night convenience stores were available but I didn't enjoy such places. At 4 A.M. a lone clerk would seem to take cover when I entered, and I'd get the feeling he was reaching under the counter for a gun.

After a few random visits I came to admire supermarkets. I decided they are the most American of all things. This didn't strike me during the day when the stores were crowded with hurried shoppers dodging one another's carts and not even saying excuse me when they bumped you reaching for a can of soup. I liked a supermarket at two or three o'clock in the morning when I was the only customer and I could walk the aisles among all that plenty. Hundreds of thousands of dollars worth of goodness and when I was in there alone it all seemed to be mine. A few times it almost was all mine. I could fill a cart and never see another person in all those acres of groceries. Nobody was there to keep me from walking away without paying because the only checker on duty was in the back drinking coffee with the butcher and I had to go find her.

One early morning in the silence of a supermarket I noticed some chicken pot pies among the frozen foods. Something about those pies beckoned to me. They seemed homey, even though chicken pot pies were not common in any house I had lived in up to that time. I took three or four of them back to the apartment and cooked one in the oven and that began my chicken pot pie stage.

I became addicted to those pies. In their frozen state they were round and raw-doughy on top and sat in a thin aluminum bowl and they were not beautiful until you baked them, and then they were. When one was ready to eat, its crust turned an attractive pale brown and became nice and puffy and thick juices bubbled up around its edges. When you poked a fork into the middle of the crust a small geyser of goodness squirted out. Inside you'd find a thick milky gravy accompanied by delicate bites of chicken meat. Also vague hints of vegetables to argue that the pie was a healthy dish. But the best thing was the hot rich lardy crust.

So this was the first meal I cooked as a bachelor, if you will accept that thawing a chicken pot pie is cooking.

I ate those things daily for months. Sometimes twice a day. Friends would come by and I'd invite them to stay for supper if they liked chicken pot pies because I had stacks of them in the freezer. None of my friends accepted these invitations, not counting a photographer or two from the paper. Newspaper photographers never turn down food or drink if it's free.

Eating the same stuff every day that way is a guy thing. I've never known a woman who would do it, or even put up with it. But men like it. I think if God had not created girls, the world would be without napkins and tablecloths—maybe even tables. Women are the ones who want to make something gentle and romantic about meals. They want soft music and candles and half a dozen different forks and knives and spoons and the men go along with this because otherwise they might not get fed. But if you leave men on their own, they tend to revert all the way back to cave times. They'll eat meat out of the pot it's cooked in, and may even stand at the stove while they're doing it, and if it's the same kind of meat they had the day before, they don't care.

I used to drive out to the little town of Westoff, southeast of San Antonio, to visit the Texas artist Buck Schiwetz. He was living alone and working in a converted gas station on the Steen Ranch. Getting close to age seventy-five. Buck was most interested in whatever I brought to drink but sometimes he did cook and I was fascinated by his bachelor eating habits.

He and I got acquainted in the fifties when I was editing a house magazine for Humble Oil & Refining Co., which became a significant part of Exxon. Buck was a partner in the ad agency that lived off the Humble account. I always felt he was miscast as an ad agency executive because he was an artist, by talent and temperament, and all he ever wanted to do was paint and draw.

For years he turned out beautiful watercolors and pencil sketches of old Texas homes and courthouses, and Gulf shore scenes of shrimp boats and pelicans and gulls. Humble reproduced these in its company magazine. Then it printed great volumes of the pictures and gave them away, for purposes of public relations. The result is that today, framed Schiwetz prints hang in thousands of Texas homes. My guess is that most of the people who see these pictures daily don't even know who Buck Schiwetz was. Yet it's my belief that he did as much as anyone to introduce decent art to the families of my state.

Sometimes when I'd go to see Buck at Westhoff I'd stop in Cuero and pick up half a dozen T-bones. At supper time he'd bring out two skillets and slap a steak in each one and turn the gas up high as it would go and give the meat a thorough scorching. Then he'd sit down with one skillet and hand me the other and we'd eat steak, out of those skillets. He might have a loaf of bread and a can of beans, and he might not.

Schiwetz had lived in New York and he'd traveled over a lot of the world. He'd dined with corporate CEO's and university presidents and attended many formal dinners, some of them held in his honor. But living out there in the boondocks by himself, he sometimes ate like a savage.

When he could get somebody to drive him into Cuero he'd buy a huge hunk of beef. Back at the ranch he'd put it in a paper sack and roast it in his oven. Every day he'd carve off enough for dinner and then supper and the roast wouldn't come out of the oven until it was just about destroyed. I'm talking about several days, and that meat never went into the refrigerator.

Buck died at eighty-six and the doctors said what he ate didn't kill him. Even so, I wouldn't recommend that any normal person try his system of storing meat in the oven. Schiwetz had an iron interior and could eat things that would poison you or me or maybe a small horse. And drink things that would put a mule in the hospital.

———

The chicken pot pies never got old for me. I quit them because when I went for a checkup my doctor told me to get off those things, that they were loaded with fat and were making my cholesterol go up and weren't helping my blood pressure, either. He said I needed to eat vegetables.

He didn't say what color of vegetable so I decided to start cooking pinto beans. Along with black-eyed peas, pinto beans kept me alive during the Great Depression, as we'll see in a later chapter, so I hold them in highest regard. Even though I had never cooked any pintos, it seemed simple enough. I went out and bought a twelve-inch cast iron pot, a Dutch oven, and seasoned it according to the literature that came in its box. I still have that pot and it's now midnight black and grows more beautiful as the years pass.

That pot and I cooked pinto beans, and we kept cooking them, until we got it right. In my column I wrote about the pot and about doing those beans and received favorable notice from several readers.

A couple of weeks later people who had failed to clip the bean column wrote in and asked for my recipe. I was amazed, and really pleased. This was my first attempt at serious cooking, in my own kitchen and without female supervision, and I had produced a dish that intelligent citizens liked, and wanted the recipe for it. I was encouraged.

Pintos are the only kind of beans I've ever cooked. I'm also fond of the large butter beans, the size of a quarter, but they're just fine the way they come in a can and only need heating.

In the country long ago we ate pintos almost daily and called them red beans but they aren't the reds you get in the Cajun dish called red beans and rice. That's a different bean, bigger and tougher.

Pintos seemed to have fallen from grace in the last twenty years. They're considered sort of low-grade fare. You go to a banquet and you might get black beans on your plate and you might even get red ones but you won't get pintos. Pintos are served in Mexican cafes sometimes and they're a regular side dish in barbecue joints.

I'd like to tell you how I fix my beans.

## *Pinto Beans*

To begin with, I never try to cook any less than three and a half cups of pintos. These beans usually are sold in two-cup packages but if you have a pot designed for four cups, two cups insults that vessel. It wants to be full so it can do what it was intended to do. My old black pot will handle four cups but it gets crowded when the other ingredients go in, so I fix just three and a half.

And I still look the beans. Meaning you pour the dry beans out on a table and examine them and sort them and discard anything that's not a bean. Like little clods of dirt and small sticks. Sometimes during the handling a bean will separate at its seam and these half beans are all right to cook but I cull them because they don't look nice in the pot. Dry beans are marketed a lot cleaner than they used to be because machines have been invented to remove most of the trash. However, now and then you find a pebble that could take a filling out of a tooth if you crunched down on it really hard.

You need to wash your beans well. I've watched camp cooks dump pintos in a pot without ever washing them but you'll see they need washing after you pour off the first rinse water. It'll look like what's left over in the tub after a field hand's Saturday night bath.

Directions on the package will probably tell you to soak pintos overnight but I quit doing that because it's not necessary and it's too much trouble. And some beans get soft with all that soaking and tend to cook into a mush. I cover my beans with half an inch of water and when they swell up, I keep adding water to cover. Two to three hours is plenty of soak time. In fact, you don't really have to soak 'em at all but I like to do it because I think it makes the beans better and I enjoy seeing them take on that water and puff up so pretty.

Put the beans on the stove in the same water you used for soaking, and add enough water to cover them maybe an inch. Get the pot up to a rolling boil. Then turn down to simmer and don't ever let the pot reach a high boil again. Just keep the liquid moving a little. Now pitch in a big onion, cut in quarters, and a generous chunk of salt pork. Take a butcher knife and put several deep wounds in the salt pork, to make the flavor available. When I cook beans just for myself I don't use the pork because I'm supposed to be on a low salt diet but most people want that good old salty-greasy flavor in there and I hear that well enough.

When the pot calms down from its rolling boil, make a little paste out of water and maybe an ounce of chili powder, and work that in among the beans. I've never been able to put too much chili powder in beans but I'm trying to be conservative here. I also put in three or four cloves of garlic and three nice fat fresh jalapeno peppers. Whole peppers, not chopped. If things work out right, those jalapenos and the chili powder give the beans just a kiss of heat on the tongue. I love hot peppers and raise them in pots as a hobby and eat at least one every day. I'm not interested in getting a blistered tongue, though. I want the flavor more than the heat, but you can't have one without a little bit of the other.

That's about all I put in the pot, except after about an hour I dice up another big onion and stir it in. You'll never see any of the dices when you eat the beans because they'll die in the juice but they make their contribution. Salt? I never salt beans until late in the game, and maybe never. You've got that hunk of pork in there, and the chili powder has salt in it. So wait, and taste. You can add salt last if you need it. Some people want everything they eat to be salty. I was married one time to a lady who was a super-salter and would shake salt on food that was already too salty for me. That kind of thing is hard on marriages.

You want to guard your beans while they're cooking. I've known people who'll put on beans and go off half a day and never worry. I believe beans need worrying about, and watching.

Mine were easy to watch because I seldom go to an office to work. When I wrote for the *Houston Post* I stayed home and mailed my copy to the paper. Now I write on a computer and when I get my stuff ready, I hook it up to the telephone and if I hit the right buttons it goes in a few seconds to the Great Computer at the Houston Chronicle, where I have been on the payroll since 1984. So when I was trying to learn how to cook, I was always at home like a housewife to tend to whatever I had on the stove.

The reason you need to guard your beans is that they're a

temptation. One time in a fishing camp, where a big pot of pintos was simmering on the fire, I saw a fellow come along and throw three bell peppers in those beans. This came near to causing a fist fight. The cook in charge of the beans considered the bell peppers an insult, and he wasn't able to laugh about that for two or three years.

In crowded kitchens a misguided person may come along and put something in your pot that you don't want in there. Cold water, for instance. If the beans need more juice—and I'm in favor of plenty of juice—don't ever pour in cold water. It makes the beans tough. Keep a separate pot of hot water on the stove and add juice from that. Some people pour beer in their beans while they're cooking and that's all right with me if it's warm. If it's a cold beer go ahead and drink it but don't pour it in my beans.

That recipe will serve a pretty large crowd if they insist on eating anything other than beans, so you may be wondering what one bachelor did with such a large potful. I froze them in lunch-sized containers and ate them daily with cornbread. In my early times I was exposed to the theory that pinto beans and cornbread made up a balanced meal, and I feel I have proved the theory.

My early attempt at cooking cornbread turned out pretty weak despite the fact I used those supermarket ready-mixes. Sometimes my cornbread was soft and had no more texture than a birthday cake, and other times it would collapse in the pan and get hard and I'd need a butcher knife to slice it. But as an additive to pinto beans, it was all right when crumbled up.

I decided my main problem on cornbread was that I didn't

have the proper vessel. So I bought a big iron skillet, the kind my Methodist mother used, and after that I did better, when the skillet got seasoned. Some days I'd mention in the column that I was struggling with cornbread and I ended up with two dozen cornbread recipes. The one I decided to like best came from my sister-in-law, Lou Green of Bastrop, Louisiana. The fact is, though, that I never got really comfortable doing cornbread from a scratch recipe. If I had to fix cornbread today I'd use one of those ready-mixes, which work fine if you've got the right pan and pay attention to the directions.

Lou Green is the older sister of Mary Helen, the mother of my two children. Mary Helen and I stayed married for twenty-five years before we divorced. Her putting too much salt on everything was not one of the major reasons we split, although it was on my list. She had a list of her own that was much longer than mine and evidently more convincing, since the lawyers and the court gave her everything we'd accumulated over a quarter of a century.

A number of years after the divorce, when I'd gotten together a few pots and pans in the apartment, sometimes I could catch Mary Helen in a friendly condition and she'd give me recipes over the phone. Pot roast, for instance, beef stew and a good pork chop casserole that I always loved.

My sisters came to visit and I did the pot roast and it was great. That gave me confidence and a little later on I invited two friends to supper, to show them how well I was getting along as a bachelor. I fixed the pot roast and it turned out a fatty disaster. The friends picked around in it and left early and said they had a big day tomorrow. I suspect they went out and ate at a restaurant.

After that night I tried the pot roast again a time or two but

I was never able to make it work as well as on that first night. Which showed me one of the terrible truths about cooking—that you can follow a good recipe carefully and yet it won't always turn out the way it's supposed to. Your ingredients might not be quite right, or maybe the stage of the moon figures in, or your attitude is bad.

Along about this time I tried other meat dishes. I produced a meatloaf that even I wouldn't eat, and neither would my neighbor's old cat that came around every day to see if I had done anything he liked. His name was Satan and I thought he was picky. I have opened a few cans of cat food in my life, and smelled the dead-fish mixture that cats like. Yet here was a visiting cat telling me he wouldn't eat my meatloaf.

After that I abandoned cooking meat for a long while, and stuck to vegetables. The supermarket nearest my apartment put up really beautiful vegetable displays in its produce department. Huge spreads of lettuce in half a dozen shades of green. Massive explosions of yellow squash. A great rack of broccoli with the ugly thick stems hidden and the dark green bulbous tops facing out, so the display looked like one world-record head of broccoli. That place stacked carrots in such splendid arrangements I was hesitant to pull one out because it seemed to deface the sculpture.

We're talking here about 1982, which is when I invented my Soupwich. If I am remembered for anything I ever cooked, which I doubt, it will be because of the Soupwich.

## The Soupwich

Most of the stuff I fixed and ate was originated by other people but the Soupwich was all mine. It was born one night when I brought home a few fresh vegetables and dumped them in a pot and boiled them until I thought they were done. I washed a standard soup bowl and placed a slice of whole grain bread in its bottom and poured over it a generous amount of the boiled vegetables with their juices and ate this with a large spoon.

Something about the preparation appealed to me. It seemed to combine the goodness of a bowl of fresh vegetable soup and a sandwich made with fine firm bread, so I named it the Soupwich and went back to the grocery store for more ammunition.

For weeks I tested and tweaked this recipe. I tried making it with beef but it then threatened to become stew and I didn't want a meat flavor. I needed the flavor of fresh vegetables.

I'd buy grocery cartloads of potatoes, green lima beans, butter beans, string beans, snap peas, snow peas, English peas, chick peas, cauliflower, celery, squash, turnips, corn, onions, cabbage, and lots and lots of those skinny fresh carrots with the green tops. I'm forgetting a few items but never mind.

My interest in fresh vegetables was inspired by W.D. Bedell, my editor at the *Houston Post* for thirty years. Toward the end of his time Bill had serious health problems that required him to stay on a merciless diet. One day he remarked to me that a leaf of lettuce he'd eaten had a pleasant and distinctive flavor, a comment that made me thoughtful. I had never imagined a thing like lettuce could be flavorful, or have any taste at all. But the kitchen adventures I was having with my Soupwich showed me Bedell was right. A bite of nature's greenery had a subtle and secret taste I'd never known because I'd been eating it all my life with meat and fat and salt.

At the apartment I'd get out my four-gallon San Leon pot and dump in all the vegetables I hauled from the supermarket and let that those sweethearts simmer for hours and then I'd pour 'em up and freeze 'em the way I did the beans, to make individual Soupwiches.

The individual who ate the Soupwiches was me. I have not been able to convert others. One of my neighbors offered to eat a Soupwich if I'd stop putting cabbage in it. He said the smell of cabbage was reaching to the third floor of the apartment complex. So I did leave cabbage out of the mix but I eat a Soupwich for lunch at least five times a week even now, almost twenty years after I invented it.

It pleased me that I could use an entire stalk of celery when I did my vegetables for the Soupwiches.

I have a theory that fifty per cent of all the celery brought into American kitchens is never eaten. People use a few ribs off a stalk and then they go somewhere for the weekend and the next Thursday they're fixing a meal and they want celery again. They take it out of the refrigerator and it's limp, so they pitch it the garbage.

I wanted a recipe that called for an entire stalk and the answer was in the Soupwich project. I'd put my four-gallon pot on the stove with three or four quarts of water in it and the first thing that went in there was chopped celery. By this time I'd acquired a big heavy chopping board and I loved laying things out on that pretty board and chopping them up.

In restaurants this is called prepping and it's done by lower-ranking members of the kitchen staff. While I was living in the apartment and trying to learn a little about cooking, I thought seriously about getting a moonlight job prepping in a restaurant kitchen. Because I like chopping veggies. It relaxes me.

The best chopping I've ever done was on a stalk of celery. Wash that sweetheart good and lay it out and slice off little chunks a quarter of an inch thick. One chop of the knife through the stalk gives you a handful of those pieces. I like the crispness of the cutting, the sound and feel and smell of it. You don't stop until the entire stalk has been chopped and then you pitch all the choppings in the pot. One entire stalk of celery that's used and appreciated and not a rib of it wasted. Celery has a lovely subtle nutty flavor. I've never tried it but I've long thought that a celery soup would be good, a soup that tasted more like celery than anything else. I save the tender green leaves but don't add them to the pot yet. Save for later or else they'll cook to bits and go up in steam.

Carrots next. A helpful lady at the hardware store sold me what she called a vegetable peeler, a small tool that didn't cost more than a buck. I suppose most cooks in the country have such a tool but I had not been exposed to one. I now class it one of the greatest inventions that ever lived in a kitchen drawer. Slide that tool along a carrot and it peels away the thin covering and it's such a smooth and easy and sexy procedure. Works just as well on potatoes except you better be careful or you'll peel the top layer of skin off your fingers. I must be one of the few taxpayers on the planet who likes to peel potatoes, and cut them up in chunks for the soup pot.

Then in go onions, turnips, corn, and all the beans and peas and whatever else is left. Get that big pot boiling gently and when you can smell it out in the hall, throw in a handful of peppercorns and as much salt as you think you'll need. And add two or three large cans of peeled tomatoes.

Along about this time I met a pretty black-haired woman who had divorced her husband and we became friendly. She is an educated person and so she was able to teach me a number of valuable lessons. One had to do with how to peel a turnip, and that improved my vegetable soup. A turnip needs to be peeled deep to remove a bitter layer, a sixteenth to an eighth of an inch thick, that's just beneath the skin. Cut the turnip in half and you can see the outer layer that needs to be removed. Turnips are kin to pinto beans, in that they are not counted to be really high class groceries. You won't find turnips on many fancy restaurant menus and that's a shame because this is a fine vegetable with a distinctive flavor.

This woman also introduced me to things like thyme, and oregano, and other herbs that further improved my soup. However, I must say that she has never showed much interest in eating it.

One of the secrets to a successful Soupwich is the bread. (I have been told that what I make in the great pot is really vegetable stew, and not soup. But if I accepted that ruling I'd have to call my creation a stewwich, which doesn't have the proper ring to it.) When you pour a large ladle of my soup over a slice of bread in the bottom of a bowl, you want really substantial whole grain bread. Don't use this ordinary white gummy stuff. I expect it's the most popular bread in America but used in my Soupwich it'll get soggy and taste like raw dough.

One of my several problems as a bachelor cook was that I'm a messy housekeeper. When I finished fixing a meal my little kitchen looked like a used battleground. I didn't worry about this much since most of the time I was the only person who saw the mess.

My neighbors would drop in now and then and look around and try to keep from wrinkling up their noses but they didn't stay long enough to be offended much. A nice divorced lady named Charlotte lived next door and she once offered to help me clean up the kitchen and decorate the entire apartment, which she evidently thought looked austere, or worse. This was a kind offer but I refused it because I figured I might end up with pink curtains and ruffles around the bottom of my bed.

My other close neighbor was Chico, who came in frequently to bring a book he thought I needed to read, or to borrow one of mine. Chico was not interested in cooking and didn't care whether my apartment was decorated or dirty. I will remember him forever for knocking on my door one night and asking to borrow a cup of vodka.

At this time a young fellow named Bill Shearer was struggling for profit in a small publishing firm based in the Texas Hill Country at Fredericksburg. He had published a couple of my books and when he came to Houston on business he'd bunk at the apartment to save hotel money, and sometimes eat what he found in my pantry.

Shearer was about the same age as my son, and even looked like my son, six feet tall with light brown hair and pale blue eyes. He could walk into a room and grin and make a little joke and change your day, and make it better just by showing up. He was in love with three things: Airplanes, books, and his pretty wife Kathy.

He flew airplanes from the time he was eighteen. When I got to know him he was a sales representative for Texas A&M University Press at College Station. He had a couple of kids by then and a little second-hand two-seater airplane with a tricycle gear. His ambition was to be a publisher and fly around the country in an executive jet and make a difference in the world by publishing good books.

His boss was Frank Wardlaw, a giant in Southwestern literature. For years Wardlaw directed the University of Texas Press at Austin and later established the press at Texas A&M.

Shearer loved to tell about going into Wardlaw's office to re-sign, and to say he wanted to become a book publisher. Wardlaw, a speaker in the Winston Churchill style, could read a weather report and make it sound like the Declaration of Independence. He told Bill, about his ambition to become a publisher, "The beaches are strewn with the bones of those who've tried."

But then he did all he could to help Shearer succeed, and almost everybody else with a connection in Texas letters did the same, mainly because we liked him and wanted him to make it. He sold his airplane and his home and moved his family out to Fredericksburg where he bought an old abandoned dance hall and turned it into a publishing house.

Much of his business was Houston connected so he was on the road a lot, and showed up frequently to sleep on my seventy-five dollar sofa in the apartment. The guy could sleep anywhere. He'd pull into a roadside park and read a book with a flashlight and go to sleep and spend the night. He was seldom without a book. He'd prop one on the steering wheel and read it while he was rolling seventy miles an hour along Interstate 10.

I was doing a lot of traveling then and sometimes I'd run into Bill in Austin or Dallas and if I had a motel room he'd ask to spend the night with me. That meant he'd borrow a pillow and sleep on the floor, and be up and walking out the door at five A.M. Sometimes at odd hours he'd suffer an attack of what he called get-home-itis, a disorder likely to strike him when he'd been away from Kathy for two or three nights. I've known him to rise up off my black sofa at one o'clock in the morning and say, "I've got the get-home-itis," and walk out and drive five hours to Fredericksburg.

He almost never carried money, or credit cards. He might

come to Houston to meet an author, and if he needed to take the guy to lunch he'd have to borrow twenty bucks. But he was always a welcome guest at my place, for many reasons. One was that he couldn't stand dirty kitchens. He'd walk in the apartment and look around and mutter, "My God," and start cleaning. I loved to cook after he'd finished in the kitchen because every pot and dish and cup and saucer was shiny and the knives and forks were in their proper slots in the drawers and stacked just right.

Sometimes I'd come home from a trip and the apartment would be spotless and I'd know that Shearer had been there. My neighbors might come in and see the order and the cleanliness and they'd ask who did it, because they knew I didn't, and I enjoyed telling them my publisher did it and that was the truth.

Shearer's idea of a good place to eat was the closest hamburger joint, or a pancake house (for lunch), or the most doubtful-looking Mexican food café. Which bothered me somewhat because he wouldn't eat my Soupwich. Hardly anybody I tried to feed appreciated what I fixed. They were always saying they didn't have time to eat because of an appointment, or they'd already eaten and weren't hungry, or they were on some kind of restrictive diet.

⟾

One of the best dishes I ever prepared at the apartment was my brunch omelette. See what you think about it:

### Four-Egg Omelette

Take one large black cast iron skillet and fry half a dozen slices of bacon to crispness. (I have since learned about things like omelette pans but I didn't know about them when

I was doing this dish.) Lay the bacon out on a paper towel that'll soak up some of the grease.

Break four eggs into a mixing bowl and add a cup of milk and stir gently but thoroughly. Pour off most of the bacon grease left in the skillet. You want just enough grease left in there that you can see it move when you tilt the skillet. (If I did this now I would bring out a separate skillet and use olive oil instead of bacon grease but when I was doing the omelette I was still in love with bacon grease.)

Cut up the biggest onion you can find, but don't chop it too fine. Sizzle this onion in the skillet, Keep it moving with whatever you're using for a stir tool. I hear this kind of process is known as sautéing but I'm not sure cooking onions in bacon grease would answer to that fancy name. Anyway, keep doing the onions that way until you can't stand not to taste one. Onions frying give off one of the finest aromas.

About the kind of onion to buy, I'm not as enthusiastic as some consumers about these super-mild onions developed by the plant breeders the last few years. Some of those things are so mild they don't even taste like onion to me. There's a fellow on a Houston radio station who sometimes advertises a certain kind of onion and he always says they're so sweet and mild he eats them like apples. Well, if an onion hasn't got any more kick to it than an apple I'd as soon eat a radish.

When your onion gets slightly brown scoop it out of the skillet and put it over there on the paper towels with the bacon. Dice up a good double handful of cheddar cheese and chop up two medium jalapeno peppers and add these to the goodies on the towel.

Before you pour in the eggs, check the grease in the skillet. You might need to add a little. Those eggs are going to cover the entire bottom of a twelve-inch skillet so you need a solid covering of grease. It's easy to put too much. Think this: Don't put any more grease than you want to eat because you're going to swallow everything that goes in the pan.

Test your heat by dropping in a teaspoon of the milk and egg mixture. If it sounds like water hitting a red hot stove, that's too much heat. You want the grease hot but not too. When you pour 'em in you want those eggs to give off just a whisper, not a scream.

You need a nice long egg flipper to work this omelette. Keep raising up the edges to see if the eggs are taking on body, and when their bottom is solid enough that you can lift it, quickly crumble the crisp bacon over the eggs and scatter in your onion and jalapenos and cheese and add a lot of black pepper. And salt if you think you'll need it but remember all that bacon, which is salty as the Atlantic.

Now comes the tricky part. You've got to slide your flipper blade underneath and fold half the contents of the skillet over onto the other half, like a giant taco. Then let it cook a little longer but not very because it'll keep cooking a while after you take it off the fire.

This is a big omelette and would probably feed three or four people if they had other things to go with it, but I always ate the whole thing myself, with toast and coffee. The virtue of such a concoction is that it's thick and holds its heat to the last. It's the only omelette I've ever known that didn't go cold on me halfway through the eating.

If you mess up when you try to fold half the omelette over the other half, and everything sort of collapses, don't despair. Just mix the ingredients together and call it scrambled eggs. Doing a big omelette like this may take practice.

There are those who'll mention that eating four eggs at a sitting is excessive, but these are the same people who'll go out and consume an eighteen-ounce steak with a baked po-tato slathered in sour cream, plus rolls and butter and a big salad soggy with ranch dressing. A large fresh-laid brown egg weighs maybe two ounces in the shell and I doubt four of them even after they're cooked in bacon grease offer a greater health threat than the traditional Texas steak supper.

——

During that bachelor time I ate a lot of stuff that my friends thought was outrageous and sometimes I'd write about it in the paper. I did that because the pieces I did on my cooking efforts always brought in more reader response than any-thing else I ever wrote. Not all of it was complimentary. In fact, I'm not sure the majority of it was complimentary. For a long time I saved an outstanding letter that was written not to me but to the letters-to-the-editor column. This woman wrote that I needed to be rescued because I was going to kill myself with my own cooking.

Probably she was referring not just to my four-egg om-elette stage but also to my ice cream time. I would make these nice summer treats. An example is what I called my Pint-Sized Dessert. I liked that name because it implied that it was small, and yet it was not. The basis of it was a pint of va-nilla ice cream. Hence the name.

## Pint-Sized Dessert

To make this lovely thing, you put a pint of vanilla ice cream in a roomy bowl and set it out somewhere and let it start melting. The average carton of ice cream a person buys in a grocery store needs thawing, the same as a frozen turkey. Be-fore I found this out, I ruined the handles of a couple of my best spoons trying to dig a bite of ice cream out of a carton.

Might as well have been trying to dig into concrete. I learned to anticipate my craving and take ice cream out of the freezer early, say at 6 P.M., and by 7:30 it might be edible.

When you can run a knife blade through the bowl of ice cream without significant resistance, it may be ready to eat. Chop it up and spread it out in the bowl and put on strawberries and pecans and chocolate syrup and any other sinful ingredients available. Pineapple is nice. Then put some calm music on the stereo and lean back and slowly eat until the bowl's empty.

Such a creation will have thousands of calories but understand this is supper, the entire evening meal, and that's all I'd eat until maybe ten o'clock the next morning. This pint-sized dessert satisfied my craving for that sort of thing and I might not eat another bite of ice cream for a month.

I discovered that even the most caloric desserts weren't so damaging if I ate them as a main course instead of after I'd already had a meal. And that way I could splurge and have as much dessert as I wanted. A pint of vanilla wasn't anything to what I put down when I had a real ice cream yearning. At this time I was traveling pretty well all over Texas in my work and sometimes I spent the night in fairly small towns where the restaurants aren't often wonderful. But every small town has a grocery store with a case full of ice cream. I'd get half a gallon of vanilla and a quart-sized jug of Coke and take them to the motel. Put the carton on the window ledge and let it start thawing. When it was edible with a plastic spoon I'd eat maybe a pint of it out of the carton, to make room enough to pour in some Coke to create a giant float. Coke and vanilla, an excellent flavor combo. I'd work on that, off and on, for two hours while watching a bad movie on TV, adding Coke when there was room in the carton. I couldn't eat it all so I'd store the carton in my cooler for the night. I always carried a plastic cooler on the road. Next morning what was left of the ice cream would be melted but still cold and I'd drink it for breakfast. Delicious with black coffee. Then I might not eat anything else until two or three o'clock in the afternoon. I didn't have this feast very often but it was a pleasant departure from a bad chicken fried steak.

In the summer when I was at home in the apartment if I fixed breakfast I had Grape Nuts Flakes in memory of my father. He called this cereal Kate Smith because he was a big fan of that singer and she was sponsored on the radio by Grape Nuts Flakes. Sometimes he ate it for a snack at night. "Before I turn in," he'd say, "I think I'll have a little Kate Smith."

When the first decent norther came through Houston, usually in late October, in memory of my Methodist mother I changed from Kate Smith to oatmeal. My mother must have fixed a boxcar load of oatmeal in her time. I like oatmeal well enough but I stopped ordering it in restaurants long ago because it didn't even seem to be the same dish as the oatmeal I ate when I was growing up. In restaurants it was always cold by the time it reached the table, and it wasn't smooth and creamy and comforting.

In the apartment I did a lot of experimenting before I managed to fix oatmeal the way I wanted it. I never had any success using regular oatmeal that came in the familiar cylindrical box, but finally I discovered I could do pretty well with instant oatmeal in the paper envelopes.

But I didn't follow the directions, which say put the dried cereal in a bowl, pour in half a cup of water and stir. That didn't suit me at all so I fooled around and made it better. Oatmeal is an important food and needs loving attention. Here's how I fix it now:

## Quick Vanilla Oatmeal

Of the kind I buy, one envelope of dried instant oatmeal is not enough so I open two and put the contents, with a cup of water, in a small stew pot. Set the burner on medium and stir until the mixture gets good and hot. It doesn't need cooking but a little won't hurt. Now add as much milk and sugar as you like and a couple of dashes of vanilla extract and keep stirring and control the heat so the mixture doesn't quite boil. But you want it hot. Now take the pot off the stove and eat.

If I'm in polite company I never fix oatmeal because good manners insist you serve it in a nice bowl and I don't like to do that. I eat my oatmeal out of the same pot it's cooked in because that's the only way to keep it hot. In fact, when I ate alone at the apartment and cooked anything in a small pot I always ate it out of the same pot. Not only did this keep the food hot, it cut down on dishwashing.

—◆—

Along with ice cream and oatmeal, I enjoyed a long association with Vienna sausages, and often had nice suppers consisting of these sausages cut up in a small pot of pork and beans. If I had a good onion I'd chop it into the beans and slice the sausages into delicate disks. They're fun to cut with a good sharp knife. Put them in the beans along with their juice which is loaded with fat but I was not watching out for fat very closely then.

This meal, the same as so many others I fixed, was not admired by my friends. I remember a night when I had just sat down to eat supper when Shearer came in hungry from Fredericksburg. "What's for supper?" he asked. I told him pork and beans with Vienna sausages and onion and his choice of bread, brown or white. "What is there beside that?" he asked, and I said nothing, unless he wanted to wait while I thawed out a Soupwich. He said he had to meet a fellow at the International House of Pancakes and went out and didn't come back for a long time.

What I liked about Vienna sausages was that I could buy eight or ten cans of them and that way I always had meat in the kitchen. I sometimes made a nice open-faced sandwich by slicing the little sausages length-wise and arranging them in an attractive pattern on a slice of bread. With sweet pickles laid across the meat. If I was out of bread I'd use saltine crackers, with one split sausage per cracker and two slices of sweet pickle. I thought this made a nice sort of canapé. One evening when I was trying to get better acquainted at the apartment I invited several neighbors over for drinks and laid out a generous tray of my crackers and split Vienna sausages with sweet pickles. Two or three of the guests commented that they were interesting. People were always saying that about my food, that it was interesting. I took this as a compliment, even though few who made that remark ever ate much of what I fixed.

———

In a previous life when I was married and raising children, I had cooked hamburgers in the back yard so I knew a thing or two about that. How not to buy what's sold as hamburger meat because it's way too fat and contains gristle and angels in heaven know what else. So now and then I'd buy lean-ground beef and do hamburgers for myself and I became so particular about them that I quit eating burgers any-where except at home.

## Skillet Hamburgers

I like a thin patty, not these thick globs of meat that a lot of people call hamburger patties. Some of those things are the size and shape of a cue ball, and can't possibly fit neatly be-tween the halves of a bun. In hamburgers, neatness counts.

So I'd make patties nice and wide and certainly not more than half an inch thick and cook 'em in my black skillet. One thing I didn't do in all the years I lived in that apartment was pollute the atmosphere by cooking out on the patio with charcoal. That may be my greatest contribution toward im-proving the environment.

I like soft hamburger buns but I don't want them cold. So I found out how to loose-wrap buns in foil and get them hot in the oven but not crusty. While that's going on you get all your ingredients ready. What I want on a burger is meat, onion, lettuce, and tomato. I don't put mustard on a hamburger and I don't put pickle and I don't put cheese. Like any person of sound mind and taste I like cheese but I don't want it on my hamburger.

In my cooking and eating experience, I've been criticized for a lot of reasons but the one I hear most often is about hamburger and mustard. Even beloved friends tell me it's unAmerican to put mayonnaise instead of mustard on a hamburger. I've been told a thousand times that a hamburger with mayonnaise instead of mustard is eaten only by girls and is often called a sissyburger. Let the critics rave. I don't care.

Mustard gives an acid taste that I don't like on a ham-burger. Sour pickles, the same. I'm also picky about the way a hamburger is put together, and the form of its ingredients. I don't often buy burgers at fast food places because they chop the lettuce, and you can't hold the burger without pieces of the lettuce falling out and scattering across your lap. Most fast food places do onion the same way. And I understand why they do it. It's cheaper.

I don't want cheaper. I want thin-sliced onion on my hamburger, and I want leaves of lettuce laid in there. None of that chopped stuff. Then tomato? If you don't have pretty red ripe tomatoes, just leave tomatoes off. I hope I've had the last hamburger made with a tomato that's not even red yet, and has no more flavor than a green gourd. We have now in the United States people old enough to vote, if they'd bother to register, and they still don't know what a ripe tomato tastes likes.

If you're building a hamburger for me, cook the patty medium done in the skillet, seasoned to taste as the cookbooks say. Take a soft hot bun out of the oven and split it and plop the two sides down in the skillet, on top of the juice left from the grilling. Let them stay just long enough that they have a suggestion of a crust on the cut side. Apply a thin covering of mayo to the buns. Lay a cover of lettuce leaves on top of the mayo. Then put on the meat. Next lay on slices of onion, and next tomato, and then another layer of lettuce before you put the top half of the bun on. Press gently. Main thing to remember is not to let the meat touch the mayonnaise directly.

My friends like this way of making a hamburger well enough, except that they want mustard instead of mayo. I see people putting ketchup on a hamburger but I don't know where they come from. Another planet probably. But as the old man said when he kissed the cow, everybody to his own taste.

―

Experimenting with hamburgers and other kinds of sandwiches is fun, when you don't have critics standing around to find fault.

One afternoon when I had skipped lunch I developed a serious hunger and could find very little edible in my kitchen. But I found bread and onion and peanut butter and I used those to make a sandwich that surprised me with its goodness. Later on when I hadn't any onion, I made the same sandwich and laid inside it a few flat pieces of potato chips and they provided a delightful crispness that I had never known in a peanut butter creation.

Those potato chips were stale but by that time I had learned to freshen chips by spreading them out on a cookie sheet and leaving them in the oven a little while at 350 degrees. Then setting them out to cool. Dry cereal can be crisped by the same method. I freshened up several boxes of corn flakes that way, and a couple of Kate Smiths as well.

―

After I'd been in the apartment maybe three years the manager sent me a notice that workers would be coming around to install a microwave oven in my kitchen. I told him I didn't know anything about microwaves and didn't want one. The oven in my kitchen was a standard electric job and I was getting along with it all right. Manager said I would have to take the microwave anyway, that the apartment owners had decreed that every unit in the complex was to have one of those ovens. I argued that I was afraid of the things, and wasn't sure they were good for my health, so the workers could just pass me by and that would save the owners some money.

The manager then gave me a lecture on how the apartment business works. The average stay of a tenant in that complex was something like two years. Incoming tenants were young and accustomed to all manner of electronics in their kitchens and they wanted microwave ovens because they were working people and they had to get up and fix breakfast quick and run. If my apartment didn't have a microwave, and if I moved out, the manager couldn't rent the place until he called out an installer to put in one oven, and that was expensive. So, I had to take the microwave.

"You'll love it," the manager said, "for thawing out your chicken pot pies."

I wonder now how he knew about my chicken pot pies. Probably he had smelled them, since my apartment was near his office. What he didn't know was that I had already passed out of my chicken pot pie stage and was into Soupwiches.

The microwave was never of any use to me, although I lived with it for seven more years. I remember using it only once. I'd seen people who drink instant coffee use a microwave to heat water in a cup and then spoon in the coffee and stir, and that did seem quick and easy.

At the time I was drinking out of a thick mug I'd been given as a reward for making a polite appearance and saying a few words at Alvin Community College. I liked the mug because once the coffee in it got hot it stayed hot, at least longer than a regular cup. Most of the time my coffee got cold before I got it drunk, so what I needed was a way to heat half a cup of coffee. One day I put that mug half full of cold coffee in the microwave and hit the switch.

I'm not saying the result was an explosion. It was more like some kind of electrical display, with sizzling sound effects and sparks and impressive tongues of fire zipping in and out of the coffee mug. I learned that the lettering on the outside of the mug was applied in metallic paint and the microwaves of the oven produced a spectacular reaction when they struck that metal. I never used the oven again.

It goes to show how much my apartment manager knew about microwaves. My chicken pot pies sat in aluminum trays. If I'd tried to thaw them in a microwave...

On my first birthday after I entered bachelorhood I received three cookbooks as gifts, from relatives and friends, and after I started writing in the paper about my kitchen adventures I was sent several more. Most were review copies from publishers who hoped I'd mention the titles in the column.

I never did that because I couldn't get a lot of benefit from cookbooks. In fact, I can't remember ever having one of those books open to follow a recipe while I cooked. I said that at a party one time and a lady remarked that no cookbook would ever include recipes for the kind of things I fixed. I told her I took that as a compliment and she rolled her eyes and walked away.

Every time I got a new cookbook I'd check to see if it had directions for boiling a chicken, and not one of them ever did. Sometimes I'd find a chicken and dumplings recipe but it would just tell me to boil one chicken. I wanted to know how, exactly, because I liked boiled chicken and I was having trouble doing it right.

## "Beamed" Chicken

Eventually I learned that I was putting too much water in the pot. You sure don't need to cover that bird with water. It's not like boiling eggs. Just a couple or three inches in the bottom of the pot is enough, and then keep the lid on. I thought of a name for this method of cooking—beaming, a cross between boiling and steaming. A beamed bird gets nice and tender but its meat doesn't fall off the bones. I sprinkle that baby with thyme and black pepper and salt and throw into the water a couple of celery ribs, chopped. Let it suffer in there until it's tender and then set it aside to cool. A lot of the fat will rise and you can skim it off and get rid of it.

Something about the flavor and texture of boiled chicken really appeals to me. I tried roasting chickens a time or two but I'd never get them out of the oven at the right time and they'd be half raw, or else way too done and dry as shucks. I ended up beaming a chicken just about every week and eating on it a couple of days. That tender meat makes great sandwiches. And I kept hearing that I ought to save the liquid in the pot because chicken stock is good for flavoring lots of dishes. So I always saved it but I never used any that I recall.

It sounds a little weird but I grew to enjoy cleaning every last bit of meat off a chicken carcass, until there wasn't anything left but a skeleton which I always gave to that Satan cat. I never cooked a chicken without that cat's showing up on my patio and waiting for it to get done. I'd give him the skin and the liver and gizzard but he wouldn't leave until the bones were served.

People tell me now I shouldn't feed bones to a cat, or a dog, either, so I don't recommend it. But on dogs, I've sure mauled that rule. My old dog Jiggs that I grew up with got all the bones ever gnawed under our roof. On Sunday when we had fried chicken somebody would always say, "Save your bones for old Jiggs." One time he got in trouble by catching and eating an entire fryer—feathers, feet, head and beak—so

I figured a few cooked chicken bones weren't any strain on him. He'd chew 'em up like potato chips.

As a consequence of my cooking, that Satan cat and I worked into a friendship at the apartment. He came to visit almost daily and sometimes provided entertainment by getting in a loud scrap with a yellow tomcat from across the street. They'd fight on the metal roof of the carport just outside my window and those dudes would roll and yowl and thump and their eight sets of claws scratching on that tin roof, man, neighbors would come out of their apartments to see what the racket was about. It was a wonderful noise.

———

I have to say I enjoyed my years in that little apartment. The rent kept going up, as rents have a habit of doing, but I still miss some of the aspects of apartment life. I have a pleasant memory of the time my dishwasher decided to quit getting the dishes clean, and I went to the office and reported the matter. The next day two maintenance guys came and installed a new washer. One time a fierce rainstorm flooded my patio and water ran under the sliding glass doors to soak my carpet and the manager sent a fellow with a great machine to siphon up the wetness and dry the carpet. If a faucet in the bathroom leaked, a man came to fix it. If a drunk threw a beer bottle out of a passing car and broke one of my windows, which in fact did happen, here came a guy to put in new glass. I liked that system. I think about it now when I call a plumber and he walks away folding my $300 check into his shirt pocket. And when I pay a yard man $40 to mow the grass.

Something else I liked about the apartment was the exposure it gave me to ethnic variety. Houston's population includes representatives from almost every ethnic persuasion on the planet, except maybe Eskimos. I once met a woman from Tasmania, working in a Houston tailor shop.

A big apartment complex draws a wonderful concentration of people from all over the world. For a while our chief of maintenance at the complex where I lived was a gruff dude who introduced himself as a "redneck from East Texas." (I befriended him with a bowl of pinto beans and a hunk of cornbread. He said it was pretty near as good as his mama used to cook up in Angelina County.) His assistant was a grinning kid from Vietnam. The apartment manager was an Italian-descended fellow from a farm in the Brazos River Bottom. Working in his office was a sharp young lady immigrated from Germany. We had employees from Africa, Mexico, England, and they seemed to get along all right. I felt that was encouraging.

The variety was even greater among those who lived in the apartments. Sometimes you could walk along the halls late in the day and record the smells of cooking food and make a good guess about where the residents originated. The Indians out-smelled us all—Indians from India, that is, with their curries. The aroma drifted down the halls for half a block and dominated even my big pot of vegetables before I stopped putting cabbage in it.

My apartment had a narrow thirty-foot patio that received half a day of direct sun. Flowerbeds ran the length of the patio on two sides so I had sixty feet of planting space. I grew hot peppers out there, because I needed peppers for my Soupwiches. I also planted an extraordinary vine called an air potato. (The Irish potatoes you eat daily are root vegetables, formed underground below the above-ground vine. I add this because I meet people, fully grown, who aren't sure where potatoes come from. Like maybe they're manufactured by General Foods.)

Air potatoes are edible and I did intend to eat them when I planted the vines. However, what I did mostly was stand around in amazement at how fast the vines grew. They produced leaves up to ten inches wide and the main stems climbed upward at a rate of six to eight inches a day.

My apartment was on the ground floor of this three-story complex. One afternoon the young couple that lived above me called down and said my vines were passing their balcony and going on up to the third floor. Three days later I heard from the third-floor occupants who said one of the vines had tried to grow into their living room. They had pushed it out and closed the balcony doors. It ended up on the roof of the complex where it captured a couple of TV antennae.

I planted those vines for three or four years and they climbed all over the building and finally I quit growing them because some people didn't want the things snaking around their balconies. I always meant to cook some of the potatoes they produced, hanging off their sturdy runners. But I was doubtful about eating the fruit of a vine that aggressive.

My hot peppers were a social advantage, however. I grew them in pots and I had several kinds. Jalapenos, of course, and cayennes and the little chiltipiquins and the super-hot habaneros and those big hot longhorns that make great chile rellenos. The Hispanic fellows who mowed the yard and took care of the flowers and shrubs would water my peppers when I was gone and we'd divide them up when they were ready to pick. Peppers are a good way to make friends.

The complex was a wonderful place for a person in the writing game. All manner of sights and sounds and smells. Loud arguments in the middle of the night. Parties down the hall. People having heart attacks or strokes and being hauled off to the hospital at two A.M. Once we even had a fatal shooting. A resident was causing a disturbance and a cop came and the two of them fought, even fell into the swimming pool and wrestled there, and the policeman finally shot the guy dead not fifty feet from my front door. Unfortunately I was not home that night and missed all the excitement.

I remember other disturbances. The young couple who lived in the apartment above me for about a year often made love in such a boisterous manner, I would have been justified in making a complaint to the office, and I might have if the racket hadn't so interesting. I assume that they were making love. The bumping and thumping and whining and squealing seemed appropriate to that activity, but sometimes it was hard to say whether they were loving or fighting. I think the former, because I doubt any couple would fight that long. Or that often.

When I moved I went to a better and a lot quieter place. The last thing I saw when I left was that old Satan cat, sitting on my patio fence, waiting for me to boil another chicken. A month later I drove by there and he was hunkered down on the roof of the carport, looking sort of gaunt.

## Lou Green's Cornbread

Here's how Lou Green gives directions for this recipe:

*¾ cup corn meal*
*¼ cup flour*
*1½ tsp. baking powder*
*1 tsp. salt*
*1 tsp. sugar*
*¼ tsp. soda*
*1 egg*
*1 cup buttermilk*

*Heat small skillet with ⅛ inch of oil in 450-degree oven. (Cook all bread in hot oven.) Stir cornmeal, flour, baking powder, salt, sugar, and soda in mixing bowl. Goosh it all around. Add maybe half the cup of buttermilk. Stir more. Add the egg and the rest of the buttermilk until batter is thicker than pancakes. Put in two tablespoons of the hot oil out of the skillet. Stir batter just a little more. Pour batter in skillet, cook until light brown and firm. Then flip it and cook about three minutes more.*

## *Mary Helen's Pork Chop Casserole*

When we first started eating this, cream of mushroom soup was a new invention.

> *6 to 8 thin pork chops*
> *1 cup of rice*
> *1 can cream of mushroom soup*
> *1 package onion soup mix*

*Pour half the package of soup mix over the rice in a long shallow baking dish.*

*In separate bowl, mix the can of cream of mushroom soup with two soup cans of water, heat slightly, then pour over the rice.*

*Layer in the pork chops.*

*Sprinkle remainder of onion soup mix over pork chops and add black pepper to taste. Cover with foil.*

*Cook in oven approximately one hour at 350 degrees. Remove foil. Let cook down until rice "sets up."*

## Mary Helen's Pot Roast

Two pounds of beef roast, chuck or shoulder, fat trimmed
2-3 T. oil for browning
Flour, for dusting
4-6 cups of water, in saucepan
1 large or 2 medium onions
1 clove of fresh garlic (optional)
1 bunch fresh carrots
2-4 ribs of celery, diced
1 can whole tomatoes
1 bay leaf
1 tsp. dried thyme
Salt and black pepper to taste

Heat the oil to sizzling.

Season the beef with salt and pepper and dust with flour; brown in hot oil until meat is seared on all sides, pour off excess oil.

Boil water in separate saucepan; keep hot; return to boiling just before use;

Peel and slice onions; peel carrots and cut crosswise into thick slices; peel and mince or crush optional garlic.

Add vegetables to pot with meat and brown lightly.

Add can of tomatoes with juice, breaking up tomatoes gently with fork.

Sprinkle meat and vegetables with thyme; add bay leaf.

Add boiling water so it comes halfway up the meat. Lower

heat so water simmers; cover partially. Add water, if liquid gets too low.

Cook until meat is tender. Remove bay leaf.

Thicken juices for gravy as follows:

Blend 2 T. flour in cold water; add hot liquid from pot until "flowable" and stir into pot juices; let cook fifteen additional minutes.

# The Early Times

*T*he first thing I remember eating was a bowl of oatmeal. Before that, I surely must have had a good deal of food but I can't recall any of it. How old I was on the day of the oatmeal I don't know but I was sitting in a grownup chair with something under me. A couple of pillows, probably, to give me enough elevation to get my mouth a little higher than the rim of the bowl.

My eyes, then, were an inch or so higher and I can still see the smooth creamy surface of the oatmeal in that bowl, and this was more than seventy years ago.

The reason I remember eating the oatmeal is that I was bragged on for doing it. My father watched me spoon it down and he grinned and reached over and rubbed my head. His great hand covered my skull and I loved the feel of it because it was a love rub.

That gesture from my father was one he would repeat a thousand times in our house. For me it became the signal that things were all right, that we'd make it, no matter how tough the times were. And times got tough indeed in my growing-up years, during the Great Depression of the 1930s. When we were at home and gathered at the table and there was enough to eat, my father was at peace, and so therefore was all the family. I think these were the times when food for me became not simply a way to survive. It came close to being a family religion.

In 1945 when I came back from Europe after World War II and spent the first night at home, I was waked up at 7 A.M. by the aroma of bacon frying, and the laughter of my parents in the kitchen. During the war they had gotten up at five o'clock every morning, to read and worry about the fighting and the casualties. But once I was home they had rested well for the first time since I went overseas. The reason they were laughing, they had slept all the way to 6:30.

My Methodist mother fixed eggs scrambled with bacon crumbled in, and biscuits and skillet gravy and blackberry jelly and my father said to me, "It's sure good to see you eating like this."

After that obligatory visit I went on into the world to work and have my own life, but every time I came back home for a visit he would say that same thing, about how it made him feel good to see me eating that way. And finally I was able to understand what that meant to him.

---

The town where I had that first bowl of oatmeal was Stephenville, the county seat of Erath County, which is in what most people call Central Texas. From Stephenville we moved on west, to little towns called Hamlin, and Stamford, and then to Fort Worth so my sister could attend Texas Christian University.

In Fort Worth I was exposed to a lot of food I'd never

tasted, including hot tamales we bought from a Hispanic fellow who stood every night beside his covered cart near the railroad. When he lifted the cover, steam rose out of the cart and the tamales were still hot when we got home and they cost a dime a dozen. We ate them with saltine crackers and ketchup. I remember one night I ate seven tamales and my father rubbed my head and grinned and said it was good to see me eating that way. I was in the first grade then.

We lived on a street called Bewick and I think of our stay there as the family's big-city time. I learned to play baseball on vacant lots and tin can shinny in the street. Shinny is a game similar to field hockey but instead of a ball the players hit a tin can with sticks, usually sawed-off broom handles. It's a dangerous activity. After the can was hit a few times it became battered into a compact missile that could create serious wounds with its metal projections. I still have small faint scars on my shins from those Fort Worth shinny games.

I learned to eat duck eggs on Bewick Street, which was in a fully-developed residential area where the law would not let my father keep a milk cow. This was a serious disappointment to him because my father felt that every home, no matter where it stood, ought to have at least one cow in the back yard. We did not need a cow at this time, since milk in the stores was selling for as low as a nickel a quart. That didn't matter to my father. He wanted a cow anyway. He also wanted chickens, and the law forbade those as well. But he found out it failed to mention ducks, so he brought in a few mallards and we had duck eggs.

Apparently we didn't eat them fast enough for they began hatching and we ended up with a yard full of baby ducks. We sunk a wash tub in the ground and filled it with water so the baby ducks could learn to swim. All the neighbors thought they were cute until they got about half grown and began waddling around the neighborhood, digging in flowerbeds and crapping on the sidewalks.

We had to go out of the duck business when we left Fort Worth and moved to the little town of Glen Rose.

A couple of days before we left, all the ducks disappeared. My sister Ima Ruthie went into temporary grief because she loved every one of those creatures and had given them all cute names. They would come and climb into her arms and listen with great interest while she spoke duck-talk. My father told us where the ducks went. He said he had found a nice home for them, a beautiful place in the country where they could swim not just in a wash tub but an entire lake, and people were there who would love those ducks and feed them and they would live long happy lives. Ima Ruthie stopped crying long enough to ask if our father had told the new people the names of the ducks and he said yes, he had done that. He was a person who tried to tell the truth as often as possible.

Today if I had to guess, I would say my father took those ducks and sold them to a poultry buyer, to get enough gasoline money to leave Fort Worth.

—

In Glen Rose I began to understand the psychological significance of food. We went there for the same reason we were always moving in those Depression times—to get a cheaper place to live. We got into half a house where we had part-time use of a kitchen and a quarter of an acre of ground where we could plant a garden. People going hungry during the Depression is an ancient story but I was getting old enough along about then to understand it, to see it happening, and this put a permanent crease in my memory. I used to sit on the front steps of that old house and families would come along with empty sacks to ask if they could go in our garden and pick a few peas.

These were cowpeas that we raised—black-eyes, cremes, and crowders. I have Yankee friends who will eat a spoonful of black-eyed peas for luck on New Year's Eve but they often look as if they're taking a dose of medicine. Cowpeas are considered livestock feed by many Americans. But these peas are staples in the diets of multitudes of Southerners and Southwesterners. The older ones, especially.

In the hard times we were going through at Glen Rose, home-raised peas must have prevented serious hunger in the homes of down-and-out families. They were easy to grow, and the vines produced heavily. The gardener with the blackest thumb could spade up a plot and plant a few rows of peas and harvest significant groceries.

One of the earliest chores I can remember was helping my parents shell peas. This was often a family activity, all hands sitting in a circle after supper and talking about what happened during the day. My favorites were the crowders when the pod had fully matured. The crowder is a large pea and easy to shell. Snap off one end of the pod. Pull the string down until it breaks off. Open the pod with the fingers and push the seeds out with the thumb, into a bowl held on the lap.

Black-eyes usually were a little harder and slower and cremes were the toughest because they're a small pea in a tight pod, often difficult to get open. But cremes were always our family favorite on the table-cooked much the same way we did pinto beans, with a chunk of salt pork. But eaten with a sweet relish or a sprinkling of celery salt. And yellow corn-bread and butter.

Understand these were green peas, right out of the garden. A bushel basket of them in the hull would shell out to make several messes, for probably eight to ten meals.

But we also shelled and saved dry cowpeas. The pods were picked when they were yellow and shriveled and you could hear the peas rattling inside them. Some farmers planted large plots of black-eyes that were left to dry in the field and hand-picked and hauled in by wagon. These were not shelled by hand, but threshed in a primitive way that was hard work but an entertainment to watch.

It was done on a windy day. Each thresher would fill a bur-lap bag—what we called a tow sack—with dry peas and he would slam the sack against the fence or the barn to crush the hulls. A wagon sheet was spread on the ground. The thresher would stand on the sheet and hold his bag high and let the contents feed into the wind. The idea was that the breeze would carry away the light crushed hulls and the heavier peas would fall to the wagon sheet. Then they were gathered and stored in wooden barrels for the winter. Not for cow feed, no way. For human consumption. For suppers on cold February nights.

## *Fresh Cowpeas*

Here's how we cooked fresh cowpeas. Put the shelled peas into a big pot, cover them with water. Throw in a fist-sized hunk of salt pork, scored in several places, and a large onion, quartered. Add black pepper, if you like, and boil 'em until they are soft. Toward the end of cooking you can add more salt, if needed.

⟶

I went to school one year in Glen Rose and hated it. I'm not even certain what grade I was in. I suppose it was the second. The teacher seemed mean, and the kids were not friendly. I still think that school had a higher percentage of bullies than any I ever attended. My mother told me to tough it out, that we wouldn't be there long. But I didn't want to go to that school. I'd already attended a couple of different schools during the family's wandering and I wasn't too swift about adjusting. Every time we had recess there at Glen Rose I was tempted to run away and go home, and a time or two I almost did.

The reason I didn't was that every day my Methodist mother put a certain treat in the lunch that I carried to school in a brown paper sack. It was a fried pie.

Now a fried pie is a lot of trouble to make. But that woman was up before dawn every day, and when I was ready to hike off to school she had made fried pies and put one in my lunch sack. A pie of this kind was an incredible treat in those tough times, and I worshipped the very sight of one. It was made of a thick lardy crust folded over a stuffing of fruit and fried. Apricot was my favorite. The pie was in the shape of a half circle and the size of a human hand when the fingers are extended and held tight together. It was maybe three-quarters of an inch thick. Sometimes today I buy burnt almonds and they are the color of the fried pies my mother made.

Nothing edible I can think of now is hotter than a fried pie when it comes out of the skillet. All that runny fruit in its middle is dangerous to bite into unless you let it cool down. I had about a mile to walk to school and sometimes I tucked my lunch sack under my arm and all the way I could feel the heat of that pie against my ribs, and it would still be warm most of the morning in class.

It smelled wonderful, too. A little greasy, like kitchens smelled then, and the apricot filling gave off a particular aroma I loved. Some days I sat in class and thought more about fried pies than I did the lessons. At noon I'd go out to the edge of the school ground and hide from the bullies and enjoy that pie. It might be squashed enough to make cracks in the crust and some of the filling would be oozing out but I didn't care because to me that pie meant home.

There in Glen Rose I discovered a high truth: When you want to be home but can't, having something from home to eat is a comforting substitute.

—

From Glen Rose we moved to Grandma Hale's farm out west of Fort Worth, near the Palo Pinto-Erath county line. I was thrilled with this move because I liked the farm, but my parents must have felt totally defeated. My father was out of work and we were homeless, so we went to Grandma's. Reasons for the move were about as basic as they can get—we needed shelter and food. Thousands of families were in the same sad condition, with nowhere to go. We were fortunate that the farm was still in my father's family, and the relatives would let us go there.

We worked in the fields and did chores to try to pay for our keep. At least my parents did. What my sister Ima Ruthie and I did was run wild in the woods for an entire year. We didn't even go to school.

We hunted rabbits and chewed sugar cane and ate redhaw berries we picked on creek banks. When they were ripe and red, those berries were sweet and good. We picked and ate them off the bushes with never a thought that they might need washing. We ate mulberries and hackberries the same way. But I stopped eating mulberries off the trees when I inspected them closely and saw that every berry was alive with tiny bugs. I wonder how many thousands of bugs we ingested in those carefree times.

Most families had a watermelon patch that produced far more melons than they could eat or sell. We'd go out in the fields early in the morning when the melons were cool and pull the ripe ones and drop them from overhead to smash them open. Then with our fingers we'd dig out the seedless hearts and eat them and leave what was left.

Every farm had a patch of sugar cane, harvested in late summer and hauled to a mill where the juice was squeezed out and cooked into syrup. I get a grin out of thinking about a country boy at a party in the thirties, whispering to a girl that he had a couple of joints out in the wagon. And these would be joints cut from a stalk of sugar cane, and stripped of their outer covering and ready to be chewed as a sweetish treat.

Creeks were full of catfish. Mourning doves in the trees and fields. Woods full of cottontail rabbits. Stock tanks with bullfrogs. Hollow trees with hives of wild honeybees. Nobody with initiative would have gone hungry in that country.

Although it wasn't necessary, I believe we really could have survived as wild people, eating off the land. But we didn't. We ate at Grandma's table, and minded our manners.

―――

The kitchen in Grandma's house is not so familiar in my memory because I spent almost no time in it. I'm guessing it was six feet wide and maybe twelve feet long, far too small and busy for loitering children. I remember the wood cook stove in one corner. A pantry consisting of hanging shelves with a curtain tacked over it. A small cook table. A wood box. A tall pie safe.

No running water. No sink. Just outside the kitchen door a cistern collected rain water that ran off the roof. Children were sometimes ordered to draw a bucket of water from the cistern, or go to the woodpile and chop an armload of sticks for the cook stove. I learned a kid could get praise from the women if he chopped short sticks, because they hated to reach in the wood box and find all the sticks too long to fit in the stove.

After a meal the women heated water on the stove and washed dishes in a dish pan, using lye soap made there on the farm. When they finished the dishes they took the pan outside and threw the water in the flowerbed. Nothing was wasted, not even dish water.

I've had young homemakers ask, about those spare country times, "Since they had such small pantries, where did they keep canned goods, and jars of pickles and preserves?" At Grandma Hale's, preserved foods were kept down in the storm cellar in the back yard. Some such cellars were dug large enough that a double bed was kept down in there, for the small children or old folks who might be sick. Enough space was left for the others of us to huddle together on the dirt floor until the storm passed. Entire families would go to the cellar when an approaching storm looked severe to the men, who made such decisions. I remember sitting among the potatoes that were stored down there, looking up at the bunches of onions strung from the overhead beams, and thinking of tarantulas and snakes known to make their homes in storm cellars.

Let's consider a meal I recall in Grandma's house. It's at supper time, served when the work in the field was done—after the cows had been milked, and the mules and chickens fed, and the hogs slopped, and the eggs gathered, and all the other jobs completed that need doing when the day is dying on a farm.

It was a crude table but sturdy and rectangular. I'll say it would seat ten people and give them plenty of elbow room, but elbow room wasn't always available. Chairs were lined along one side and at the ends, but against the wall was a bench that ran the table's length and this was where the children sat. You could put on the bench as many children as necessary. You just shoved them in and told 'em to scoot over. That bench was polished to a high shine by the scooting of all those skinny little butts.

Somebody will want to remind me at this point that in the old days, children often didn't eat with the adults but were required to wait and come to the table only after the grown-ups were finished. Yes, but in my experience that happened only when an exceptionally large bunch was being fed, on high occasions. These would be attended by several families who had gone forth and multiplied and created so many kids even Grandma's bench wouldn't accommodate them.

Not letting the children eat with the adults produced a popular expression, "Take a tater and wait." I think that was a theme line in a humorous poem but I haven't been able to find the title or its author. Parents might give that order, half seriously, to hungry children whining to eat. Kids whining in the background could spoil any meal, so they'd be given a little something to ease their hunger until the adults were finished.

Grandma's table was covered with oil cloth, all the time. During the day a collection of stuff vital to the next meal was kept in the center of the table underneath what we called a cup towel. You used a cup towel to dry dishes. This item seems to be called a dish towel now, but the ones I've known in recent times are not big enough to cover the collection that always sat in the middle of Grandma's dining table.

Hidden beneath the towel were all the knives and forks and spoons, standing handles-up in quart fruit jars. Also under that spread were salt and pepper and sugar and jars of pickles and relish and chow-chow and maybe a pitcher of syrup and a jar of preserves or honey and a bottle of vinegar.

Leftovers weren't put in the refrigerator because Grandma didn't have one, unless you want to count the milk cooler. This was a broad tin tray about four inches deep and flooded with three inches of water. Crocks of milk and other dairy things sat in that cool water which kept them from souring not quite as quickly as they would have if they'd stayed on the kitchen table.

When the women set the table they distributed plates and turned them upside down and then put a fork and knife and spoon on top of each plate. I never questioned why the plates were turned bottomside up but I assume now it was to keep flies from landing in them. There were always flies except in the dead of winter. During meals at Grandma's at least one woman was forever patrolling the table, waving a cup towel to shoo the flies off the food.

This one supper I'm about to describe was not served on a special occasion. It was an ordinary Tuesday or Wednesday night. Let's say eight people were seated. Two large serving bowls were put out, and they both contained pinto beans, with lots and lots of juice. If anything we ate could be called a main course, it was these beans.

Also on the table was a large bowl of turnip greens left over from the previous meal. They were cold and some of the diners passed them up. There was no meat, unless you want to count the salt pork cooked with the beans. What we waited for from the kitchen was the great iron skillet of yellow cornbread. This was made from corn grown there on the farm and ground into meal at the grist mill. It was wonderful stuff.

That was the menu, except for milk and butter. There was always plenty of whole milk, which we called sweet milk, and buttermilk by the gallon poured into roomy goblets out of large pitchers. None of us considered that this was anything other than a complete meal. On Sundays we might have meat but we didn't expect it during the week.

In those lean times we abided by a rule that the children were not to take any of the salt pork when they spooned beans onto their plates. That law of the table never bothered me because the pork had already been boiled to death. All its flavor had departed into the bean juice and what was left wasn't worth eating. But sometimes the men at the table would take some of it. I don't remember this rule being stated or explained but the kids obeyed it without challenge. I assumed the men were entitled to that meat since they did the hardest physical work.

A number of Depression myths and jokes sprung out of the bean pot and its salt pork. That chunk of hog fat became the symbol of meat scarcity during hard times. Most of the stories insist that the meat in the pot was not eaten because it needed to be used again tomorrow, to flavor another pot of beans. I used to keep up with a grinning fellow called Turkey

Gates, who lived on the Texas coast in the Wadsworth community. He once told me that during the Depression his father would lend the neighbors a hunk of salt pork to cook in their beans, but they had to promise they'd bring it back when they got finished with it.

The beans were attacked in a variety of ways. One popular method was to split a big wedge of cornbread, arrange the halves in the plate, and then spoon beans and bean juice generously over the wedges. This was satisfactory only if the beans had a lot of juice. To this day I'd as soon not have beans unless they're swimming in juice, where the flavor is.

When the women offered a plate of cold cornbread, left over from yesterday, we'd make a tasty mess this way: Take two wedges of cornbread and crumble them over your plate. Now ladle beans and juice over the crumbled cornbread, mash the beans with a fork, add whatever condiments are available and mix thoroughly. Chili powder is a good additive here. Or a chunk of onion, chopped. Or green pepper sauce. Or chow-chow.

I meet young people now who never heard of chow-chow, even though it's still found in grocery stores. Chow-chow is made with green tomatoes and onion and vinegar and enough sugar to overcome the vinegar. So it's sweeter than it is sour. I don't know what else goes into good chow-chow but it's excellent on certain dishes when you're feeling creative.

But I especially want to tell you about dessert for this meal. Country women are famous for fixing pies and cakes and cobblers and other sweet treats but at the time I'm talking about, except on particular occasions, they didn't waste sugar on fancy desserts. Sugar was something you had to go all the way to town to get, and you had to pay money for it.

The idea was, fix enough food to satisfy everybody but don't go spending money to do it.

The dessert, for those who weren't full, was more cornbread with cane syrup or molasses or honey poured over it. I've eaten a plate of that many a night, without ever having a thought that it was anything but delicious.

This was what the adults on that farm called "making out your supper." Say a guest was present, and he'd already put down a couple of plates of whatever was offered and was sitting there with his hands in his lap and still looking hungry. That's when the host would tell him, "Come on, make out your supper." Meaning have more. Have some cornbread and syrup.

The interesting thing to me about the time we spent on Grandma's farm, eating beans and peas and turnip greens and corn and oats and fruit, is that our diet then was close to what many doctors and nutritionists are telling us to eat now, to be healthy. Lots of fiber. Not many doctors would approve of all that grease we had with the fiber but most of us were super active then, running and gunning and doing from sunup to dark, so maybe we burned up that fat instead of letting it clog up in our blood vessels. Or maybe we didn't. The life expectancy then was far below what it is now.

The conventional view of America's rural scene is that of plenty, of bountiful meals. Hams from home-raised hogs. Baked poultry. Corn on the cob. Steamy servings of fresh vegetables. Great bowls of fruit. Hot rolls and butter. Home-made ice cream. Cakes and pies. In rural Texas, even during the hard times of the thirties we sometimes produced a version of that scene, at family gatherings and holidays. But the daily diet was pretty much cornbread-and-beans basic.

During the year we spent at Grandma's farm we did a tolerable amount of visiting to the farms of nearby relatives, and I remember some outstanding breakfasts in other houses. At peak work periods neighbor men would show up and stay several days to help bale hay or shock oats or work on threshing crews and they'd be fed these huge breakfasts before the sun came up.

They got meat, and eggs, recognition that they were engaged in tough and important work. The meat was mostly sausage and the eggs were fried in the sausage fat. The workers weren't asked how they wanted their eggs. They got them hard fried. The women would put out a platter with two dozen or more eggs and the eggs were flat, with the yolks broken, and fried stiff. They were cooked in grease so hot they had black lace around their edges and the men reached out with forks and stabbed the eggs as if they were pieces of over-done meat. When the platter was empty another one showed up loaded with more eggs.

There was jelly, too, and jams, and oceans of boiled coffee poured from fire-blackened granite-wear pots. Coffee was served in thick heavy cups, sitting in saucers to match.

Sometimes I stood back and studied the way the men dealt with their coffee. This remains for me one of the most curious table habits in my experience. Let our Uncle Billy Crockett demonstrate this custom. He was always present at these big breakfasts, even when he wasn't doing any of the work. His coffee would be too hot to suit him and he didn't want to wait for it to cool. So he'd tip his cup and dribble coffee into the saucer. Then pick up the saucer, lift it to his mouth, blow on it several times, put the edge of the saucer in his mouth and suck the liquid in with a loud slurping noise. Most of the country men I knew took coffee this way.

I can't think of a container to drink from that would be more awkward than a saucer. Even for young men the procedure was a challenge. The old ones, arthritic and unsteady, would tip the saucer and spill coffee on their laps and yet they insisted on staying with this peculiar custom. I don't doubt that somewhere, old men still slurp coffee from their saucers. The last time I remember seeing it was in the early sixties, in the Texan Café in Huntsville, an East Texas town where old customs die slowly.

My father used to tell this joke: An old cowboy sat at the counter of a restaurant where service for breakfast was slow. A lady came in and took a seat and waited for service, and waited, and waited. Finally the old cowboy made a courteous offer. "Ma'am?" he said. "Would you like to have some of my coffee? It's already saucered and blowed."

———

The women—this always amazed me—they seemed to enjoy the exhausting work they did to feed the harvest hands who ate as if they'd never get another mouthful. The women rolled out of bed even before the men, and built fires and boiled coffee and mixed biscuit dough and somehow stayed in a good humor the whole time.

I remember women circling the breakfast table, while the men had their heads bent to their plates with their jaws working and one of the women saying to this inattentive audience, her voice all full of music, "Come on now, boys. I want some of y'all to try my watermelon rind preserves. Y'all tryin' to hurt my feelin's?"

Toast? No, they didn't get toast. For a working man's

breakfast of this sort, the bread was hot biscuits which kept coming pan after pan from the oven of a wood cook stove and the men broke open the biscuits on their plates and poured gravy over them.

These were not the light puffed-up flaky biscuits you see now on TV commercials. They were domed-shaped, like the tops of big mushrooms and the domes were smooth and a beautiful burnt orange color. When they were overcooked, and most of them were, their bottoms were tough and dark brown and made a crunchy noise in your mouth when you bit one, even when it was hot. After such a biscuit got cold, its bottom became truly substantial, although its domed top stayed fairly soft. To break the bottom in half you might need to grasp it in both hands. I haven't seen such a biscuit in fifty years.

Exactly what made these biscuits that way I don't know. If I did I'd try to make some. In country kitchens you could open the pie safe in the middle of the afternoon and find a dozen or more biscuits in there, left over from previous meals. The women always made more biscuits than the family could eat because they were valuable as leftovers. They had an extraordinary lasting quality. Those tough bottoms were a factor in their utility. When you saw a kid coming to school carrying his lunch in a syrup bucket, you understood that some of those leftover biscuits would be in his bucket. You could take a biscuit two days old and punch a hole in the top with your finger and sort of wiggle around in there and hollow out a place and put in jelly, or peach preserves, and that sturdy bottom would hold up for hours without leaking. Show me one of these modern-day light flaky biscuits that'll pass such a test in a syrup bucket. By first recess, wouldn't be anything left of it but mush and crumbs.

Those hard-bottomed biscuits even had entertainment value, out there in the boondocks where entertainment was sometimes in short supply. One Sunday afternoon a neighboring family had come to visit and a flock of us was gathered in the yard in the shade of a chinaberry tree. One member of the visiting family was a girl about eight years old, maybe nine. Uncle Billy Crockett, who often entertained visitors, kept trying to talk to her but she was shy to the point of pain and wouldn't communicate other than shaking her head yes or no.

Finally Uncle Billy said to one of the cousins, "Delbert, how about if you run in yonder to the kitchen and bring me three or four cold biscuits out of the pie safe?" He didn't have to wonder whether the biscuits were there. They were always there. So Delbert brought three biscuits and Uncle Billy took them and held one in his right hand and began pitching it up, about a foot high, and catching it. He did this several times, the way a person might do when he's got a rock in his hand and he's thinking about throwing it if he sees the right target.

That was Uncle Billy's way of timing his performance, waiting for the audience to get quiet and pay attention. When the moment was right he said to the girl, "Now what's your name again, Honey?" And she'd duck her head and mutter, "Myrtle Jean," or whatever it was. It might have been Myrtle Jean.

Then Uncle Billy asked her, "Well, Myrtle Jean, do you see that old hound dog layin' over yonder asleep in the dirt?"

Myrtle Jean looked and nodded and Uncle Billy said, "Do you reckon I can throw this biscuit and hit that old dog in the mouth with it?"

Myrtle Jean grinned and twisted and gnawed on her sleeve

and wrapped her left foot around her right ankle and shook her head, no.

"All right," Uncle Billy said, and took a nickel out of his pocket, "if I can't do it, I'll give you this nickel."

Then suddenly he flipped his wrist and the biscuit flew up maybe ten feet high in the general direction of the dog. Understand that hound was twenty feet away and asleep, or seemed to be, when the toss was made. But that missile never hit the dirt. The hound sprung to his feet and was standing there waiting when the biscuit disappeared in his mouth.

Everybody under the chinaberry tree laughed and Uncle Billy said to Myrtle Jean, "Now watch, I can do it with my eyes shut." He closed his eyes and flipped the second biscuit, with the same result. Hit the hound square in the mouth.

Then he said, "I can do it backwards, too. Not many people in the world can do it backwards." He turned his cane chair around, faced away from the dog and flipped the third biscuit over his shoulder. The pitch was a little high and to the right but the hound moved under it with ease and took it on the fly.

The fact is that this hound made his living that way. He had a lot of competition and needed to stay ready at all times. Country dogs then survived on leftovers out of kitchens and when a biscuit or a bone was pitched off the porch, there'd be a dog in place to catch it. My guess is that Uncle Billy could have thrown all three biscuits at once and not a one would ever have hit the ground.

After his performance, he gave the nickel to Myrtle Jean anyway and it was clearly a treasure to her. All the children loved Uncle Billy. The women did too.

—

These things I'm telling you happened in Texas ranch country, cow country, but most of my people were farmers, not ranchers. They were surrounded by great pastures that belonged to somebody else and the men of our family roamed those pastures and hunted in them because the trespass laws then were not obeyed and seldom enforced. But few of my people had beef cattle. They didn't even eat beef, on a regular basis. They ran a few cows but mainly for milk. I ate in quite a few country homes in that part of the world in my early times but I can't remember ever having beef.

Those families had no way to keep fresh meat. They could go out an hour before Sunday dinner and kill a couple of chickens to fry. They could kill a hog on a frosty morning and have fresh pork for a meal or two and then cure and smoke bacon and hams and preserve meat that way. But to slaughter a beef would leave too much meat on hand, and no way to keep it from spoiling. Of course all that changed when rural electrification moved across the land and put refrigerators and freezers in country homes. In my view that has been the greatest improvement that's ever come to rural America. Electricity.

In 1995, I sat with a good-looking woman in Felidia, one of the most expensive and popular restaurants in New York City, and ate *zuppa di branzino con cous cous* (a light tomato based soup), followed by *arosto di maiale* and an almond and pear tart with cinnamon ice cream *(crostata di pero con gelato di cannella)* for dessert.

I tell you that in case by now you're thinking I never had anything to eat in my life other than cornbread and beans and my own strange cooking. Also I wanted to get that sentence on the record before I wrote this next one:

In 1936, on the bank of the Leon River in Eastland County I ate two jaybirds, cooked on a green elm switch held over a camp fire. I started to say those birds were the first meat I ever cooked but I didn't really do the cooking. My buddy Dude Wilkins did it. In fact, I believe it was Dude's idea to eat the jaybirds in the first place. I hope it was.

We were fifteen then, or close to it, and doing a lot of wandering among the scrub oaks of the Texas West Cross Timbers country. We'd borrowed a twelve-gauge shotgun from Dude's big brother and we had four or five shells. At that time we considered that hunting and fishing were the only worthwhile activities available on this planet. We had already noticed girls, and considered them, and they were interesting and wonderful but also frightening and unapproachable. So we decided that instead of pursuing girls we ought to take that gun out and shoot a cottontail rabbit or a couple of mourning doves and cook them and eat them. In retrospect I'll say that should go down as one of the weakest decisions ever made but there's nothing I can do about it now. I suppose we wanted to shoot and eat wild things because that's what our forefathers did on the frontier. Anything ever done on the frontier had particular appeal for us. We loved that word. Frontier.

The trouble was that we wasted two of our shells on fast-flying doves, which are not easy to hit, and we couldn't jump a rabbit so we shot those jaybirds. Blue jays, that is. Dude and I argued and then agreed that anybody who ever ate a dove or a quail ought to be comfortable eating a jaybird. The species are not close kin but, as Dude pointed out, they're all birds.

A jaybird looks pretty big when he's squawking in the back yard and stealing feed from other birds but after you get him plucked there's not much left. I'm saying jaybird meat would be decent fare if you didn't have anything else to eat. Dude's mother was an old-fashioned cook who kept leftover biscuits in the pie safe, even after she moved to town from the country. So we had several of her biscuits to go with the jaybird and it wouldn't have been so bad if we'd had a little salt to put on it.

---

When we left Grandma Hale's farm after a year, we moved to Eastland, about ninety miles west of Fort Worth where the land was deep sandy and farmers grew a lot of peanuts, and still do. We ate peanuts every day. We kept a bushel of them in the kitchen and I carried pocketfuls to school and so did other kids. We were still in the dark economic times of the Depression but a good thing was that the weather was kind and crops were fair and locally-grown food was plentiful and cheap.

The newspapers had pictures of sunken-eyed men standing in soup lines in the cities but I never saw a soup line in our town. The hungriest bum could go out in the country and dig peanuts or sweet potatoes out of the sand, or swipe watermelons out of the patches or peaches out of the orchards. I never saw a bum do that but I know it was done because I did some of that myself.

The first year we lived in that little town we ate so many sweet potatoes I could see them in my sleep, sweet potatoes marching in close order drill. Our mother even used sweet potatoes for home decoration. She'd put a big one in a fruit jar of water and its bottom would sprout roots and its top would make a vine. She'd tack the vine to the top of the wall and it would snake all over the kitchen, from the sink to the ice box to the stove to the cook table and back again to the sink. Visitors would come and exclaim about that vine, and brag on my mother for creating an attractive display simply by sprouting that common vegetable.

When I was living in the bachelor apartment in the eighties I tried, in honor of my mother, to sprout a sweet potato that way but I had no success. I eventually found out I was putting the wrong end of the potato in the water. It will sit there and rot if you do that, and probably begin to smell bad before you pitch it in the garbage. Later on I visited in a rural home where a woman was growing sweet potato vines like that in her kitchen and I saw they looked pretty low class. Sort of a poor woman's ivy.

In restaurants now I sometimes see sweet potatoes, or yams, on menus accompanying meat dishes but I never see them offered fried. In the thirties our mother fixed fried sweet potatoes regularly. She would slice them lengthwise and cook them in the big black skillet, I suppose in lard or maybe bacon grease. I don't recall how they tasted but I can see one of the slices now, stretching all the way across my plate. We had sweet potatoes fixed every way possible, even baked and mashed and served as a dessert with melted marshmallows on top.

Almost every night after supper we sat around and ate peanuts, hot out of the oven of the kerosene cook stove. We called them parched. They were simply roasted awhile, spread evenly on a toast pan—what we call a cookie sheet now. Anybody could parch peanuts. Even I did it. Only thing you had to watch was leaving them in the oven too long so they got too much heat and had a burnt flavor.

In addition to their natural flavor, the peanuts came out of that oven tasting a little like kerosene, or what we were still calling coal oil. I learned to like the vague aroma of kerosene rising from anything cooked on that stove. A meatloaf, a rump roast, a pot of stew, a pie or a cake. Sometimes we made what we called skillet toast. You buttered a slice of bread and plopped it butter-side down in a hot skillet and let it get brown and I swear it tasted more like kerosene than toast, but I ate it and liked the flavor. Later on when we moved to houses where we cooked on a natural gas stove, I thought the skillet toast tasted sort of bland.

If I could own only one item among the possessions my parents left behind when they died, I'd take my mother's big black cast iron skillet. That skillet taught me lessons of value. The main one was that home could change locations a dozen times, but it would still be home if you had your family and your familiar things.

I once counted up that we lived in nine different towns from the time I was born until I left home for the last time, to return only for short visits. That total doesn't include a couple of places in the country.

As a newspaper columnist I've written scores of stories about people who didn't know what moving means. Because they were getting old and figuring on dying in the same house they were born in. Maybe even in the same room. That always seemed strange to me, that people could live their entire lives in only one place. I've heard a hundred people say to me, "Lordy, I could never move from this house. I've been here all my life. I wouldn't know how to begin moving. They'll have to carry me out of here to the graveyard."

To me, moving was a normal activity. Every year or two we'd get our stuff together and go somewhere else, and this never bothered me much. You waved goodbye to friends and felt a little tug in the chest about leaving them but new friends were waiting at the next place.

The big skillet came to symbolize home to me, and family. It was always packed last, and unloaded first. When we got to wherever we were moving, our mother put some grease in that skillet and scrambled a bunch of eggs and we sat down together and ate and we were home.

In all the years gone by since those bizarre times, whenever I see an iron skillet in a store I want to buy it. I wonder now how many I did buy, but most of them have never had the loving use such skillets deserve. I mean they need to be important to families, and heated up daily so they become cured out and seasoned and black. Even the smallest children in the family need to become acquainted with such a skillet and understand its significance.

My respect for the skillet began when we arrived in Eastland. We went there because my sister Maifred got a job at the local weekly newspaper. U.S. Highway 80 ran through the middle of this town, right past the courthouse. Past the Corner Drugstore where years later I would jerk soda when I was a senior in high school. Past the Western Union office where I'd deliver telegrams on a bicycle. This town has been bypassed by Interstate 20 and if you drive from Fort Worth to El Paso now you'll never know you went past Eastland unless you watch the road signs.

To me it's an important town because my family lived there longer than we'd ever lived in one place before. However, I don't mean we stopped moving. We just moved from one house to another in the same town, at the same rate of change that we formerly moved from one town to the other.

Eastland is where our mother began feeding other people, in addition to her family. We lived in parts of rent houses and the other parts were occupied by people who ate at our table, and this is how our rent was paid when my father wasn't bringing home any money. I'm not saying he didn't work. He worked like a junkyard dog all his life but he was a salesman and during those hard times nobody was buying anything.

For a few years our mother operated a boarding house and rented rooms and fed the roomers. She fed railroad bums, as well. They'd walk up from the Texas & Pacific tracks on the north side of town and knock on the back door and offer to work for a meal. I used to stay off to the side, pretending to be busy at something, and watch those fellows eat. They always sat on the back steps and balanced the plates on their knees. They'd hold a fork in a fist, like they were grasping a hammer, or as if they wanted to keep a firm grip on the handle in case somebody might come along and take it away, and the food with it.

A scene like that, on our back steps, showed me that I didn't really know the meaning of true hunger. Despite all my family's thin times, I'd never gone hungry. Missing a couple of meals didn't mean hunger. Having beans and cornbread for supper? That's not deprivation. That would be prosperity for the men who ate on our back steps.

Those fellows off the railroad had a common physical characteristic. Their eyes seemed drawn back into their faces, the same as the people I'd seen in the newspaper pictures showing the hungry standing in soup lines. To me that hollow-eyed look came to mean hunger. Thirty years later when I was doing newspaper stories in Houston and roaming around the streets in the ragged part of town, I saw again that look on the faces of street people. They may have been drunks or drug addicts but they were also hungry.

Our father took a traveling job selling magazines to farmers and he often accepted chickens or produce instead of cash because nobody in the country had cash then. This is where all those peanuts and sweet potatoes we ate came from. Sometimes he'd bring home a bushel of wheat and take it to the mill and get it fine-ground and for months we'd eat that whole wheat as a breakfast cereal. I thought it was better than the cream of wheat that came out of the grocery store. It was pretty much the same thing, except our cereal was whole wheat, unrefined, and had a natural reddish brown color. We boiled it in a stew pot in salted water. All the time it was cooking you had to stand at the stove and keep stirring or it would lump up, but it was delicious on a cold morning with milk and sugar.

An event highly significant in my life occurred about this time, when our father brought home a couple of milk goats. You may be thinking he had a trailer or a pickup truck for hauling cargo that included goats. He did not. The goats came home riding in the back seat of his smoky old Chevy sedan. I still see him turning in off the road, grinning at me through the cracked windshield. The head and neck of a goat poked out each rear window. The general demeanor of Spanish goats is really expressive and something about the look on the faces of those animals told me they were about to make trouble in my life, and I was right.

My father was always bringing home curious things and demonstrating how they were to be cared for. Then he'd get back in that old Chevy and leave town. This is how I learned to deal with goats, to chase around town after them when they got loose. It takes a mighty sound fence to hold a goat that's not interested in staying home. I'd come in from school and one of the goats would be browsing in Mrs. Mitchell's garden and Mrs. Mitchell would not be pleased. Or the other goat would be across the road, chewing on the sleeve of a shirt hanging from a clothesline, and it was not our clothesline. Something about the starch attracted free-ranging goats. Dealing with difficult situations of this sort was educational, but if the experience was any benefit to me it's the only thing I ever learned from a goat that I now appreciate.

From those animals I found out how to milk—meaning to grasp the teats of a four-legged mammal and manipulate the fingers in ways that approximate the sucking of a young offspring. Thus causing the mother to "give down her milk," as we said. This process is now mechanized but the principle is the same, and all consumers should celebrate the process if they are in favor of going to the supermarket and buying a quart of milk. Sometimes I think people need to be reminded of where milk comes from. It comes out of udders, by way of their attached teats, which most livestock owners call tits without blushing. I have a relative in the dairy business who wouldn't say damn if he dropped an anvil on his foot but he likes to take city visitors for a tour of his farm and he makes this joke: "You want to know how I can tell how many cows I have? I count the tits and divide by four."

I confess that early in my association with goats I was pleased because they were so cooperative when it came to milking. A milker needs cooperation from a goat because she's so close to the ground the milker would have to lie on his stomach to make the udder available. But you can give the goat a little something to eat and show her an elevated surface, such as a box a foot and a half high, and she'll hop up on it and stand there munching while you squat and milk her.

Nobody else in our town milked goats, as far as I know. When I was asked at school about why we kept goats in the middle of the county seat, I always said goat's milk was healthier than other kinds and my mother was sick and needed it. My mother was not sick, thank God, or else we'd all have starved.

Our father thought goat's milk was wonderful and drank most of what I squeezed out of those two nannies. My sisters thought the milk smelled funny and wouldn't drink it. I suppose they went without milk of any kind for two years. Me, I couldn't tell the difference.

———

By this time, a year or two after we left Grandma's farm to live in town, things had begun to get somewhat better for our family. If that were not so we couldn't have bought feed for two milk goats. Also my sisters, both older than I, began having little parties and boys came and there was laughter, and popcorn balls were made and sometimes even fudge, which required store bought chocolate and lots of sugar.

Probably what my father ought to have done, when he got a little money in his pocket, was buy a better car since his old Chevy was falling apart and he had to have wheels to make his living. Instead he bought a cow. To get the cow, he traded in those two goats. My sister Ima Ruthie cried when the goats left. I celebrated.

The idea behind buying a cow to milk right there in the middle of town, was that she would give us about two or three gallons a day which was more than we could use. So we would sell part of it to neighbors and get enough cash to pay the feed bill. Also we would have milk that my sisters would drink.

I must have been eleven when we got the cow. From that

day until I was eighteen and about to go off to college, we had a cow living in our back yard and sometimes two. When we moved from house to house in that town, the cows went with us. Let's say we'd heard about a house that was better than the one we were living in. Better usually meant the rent was cheaper. My father would take us all to look at the house but we didn't go in until he walked around to the back. If he returned to the front and said, "There's a place to keep a cow," then we'd all get out and go look at the inside of the house. If there was no place to keep a cow, we wouldn't even look.

So we were deep into a sort of junior-grade dairy business. I became known as a kid who was always leading a Jersey cow around town, looking for a vacant lot where I could stake her out to graze. Keeping a cow didn't improve my social life, after I discovered the huge importance of girls. Embarrassing things were forever happening in our yard when the prettiest girls walked by. Like calves being born, right there in the 500 block of Mulberry Street. Or even worse, cows being in heat and bawling their horns off.

I did a ton of complaining about having to fool with those cows but I did reap a couple of benefits from them. One is, in 1962 I sold a magazine story that was headlined "The Chamber of Commerce Bull." It was about an adventure in dairy breeding I had when I was a sophomore in high school. My father made me lead one of our cows across town to have a date with a big red bull owned by the local Chamber of Commerce. The story covered the details of that alliance, which turned out to be a mortifying event. I got fifty bucks for the magazine piece, at a time when I needed fifty bucks the worst way. Since then I have sold that same story half a dozen times in different markets, including a couple of newspapers, and as a journalist I have become identified with that Chamber of

Commerce bull. It must be the most popular thing I ever wrote, in almost half a century of newspaper and magazine work. I have not learned to enjoy that, but I accept it.

(The tale is included in a previous book of mine, a collection of newspaper columns titled "A Smile From Katie Hattan." By the time you read this, that book may be out of print but it'll still be around in libraries and your better rare and used book stores.)

⟶

Having that livestock on the premises inspired one of my personal recipes for gaining weight. I was always a bony kid, made up mostly of skull and feet and kneecaps and elbows, and was forever trying to develop some heft. Our kitchen was generally overstocked with milk, especially when I was milking two cows, and I figured I could use it to put on some muscle.

We'd have jugs of fresh milk in the ice box, and big crocks of milk sitting out to clabber, getting ready to go in the churn and become buttermilk and butter. Milk everywhere, in its various stages. Clabber by the gallon. I meet people now who don't know what clabber is. It's what happens to whole milk when it's not refrigerated. It sours, and curdles, but remains an excellent food if it's not left out too long. When Little Miss Muffet sat on the tuffet, eating her curds and whey, clabber is what she was eating.

Even in our little country town in 1937 we had citizens who wouldn't admit they'd ever eaten clabber because it's considered such a low-grade food, even lower than corn-bread and beans and leftover turnip greens. These were people trying to escape from their country raising. Today if they're still alive I bet they're going to the supermarket and buying yogurt because of its reputation as an upscale product. But it's a close cousin to clabber. Blindfold me and set out a cup of plain yogurt and a cup of clabber and I doubt I could tell the difference.

Every afternoon when I got home from school during my cow-milking time I'd fix myself a weight-gaining cocktail I bet would make a nutritionist faint. I'd take a pint fruit jar—that's a sixteen-ounce container—and dump two tablespoons of sugar in it, followed by about a tablespoon of cocoa. Mix the sugar and cocoa together thoroughly and pour in maybe an ounce of cream and stir, to make a paste. We weren't buying cans of chocolate syrup then so I had to make my own.

The milk from that morning, and the night before, would be in jars or crocks in the ice box and the cream would be risen so I'd take a teacup and dip up enough pure cream to fill my pint jar and stir it well until the chocolate paste was nicely joined with the cream. Then I'd turn up the jar and drink the whole thing down.

I confess I drank it fast because I made this little treat on the sly, when my mother was not in the kitchen. She didn't care about the cream because we had plenty of that but the sugar and the cocoa were something else. She would have frowned about my using those because they were expensive.

Over a couple of years I must have consumed gallons of pure cream that way, without any noticeable result. I came out of high school six feet tall and weighing about 145. Maybe without the cream I might have weighed only 120. Or maybe without the cream I wouldn't have an elevated cholesterol level now.

Young people in the thirties downed lots of strange sweetish home preparations. School kids today are criticized for eating so much junk food loaded with salt and sugar and saturated fat, and some of that criticism comes from their grandparents who once ate worse. That mixture of sugar and cocoa I fixed, to make the chocolate paste for my weight-gaining cocktail? We used to mix up full cups of that stuff and spoon it into our mouths and let it dissolve. Liquid candy. It was really gross. You'd see kids that seemed to be chewing tobacco, with dark gunk leaking from the corners of their mouths. It wasn't anything but that sugar and cocoa mixture.

We also fixed an after-school treat called bread and butter and sugar. This poisonous preparation originated before sliced bread. Take one thick slice of home-baked bread. Slather it with butter about a quarter of an inch thick. Then distribute half a handful of sugar over the butter. The calories in one piece of that stuff must have approached five hundred, yet I remember seeing kids not yet in junior high eat two slices of bread and butter and sugar within half an hour after they got home from school.

Along about this time I discovered mayonnaise, and fell in love with it. There was an evil preparation called sandwich spread, or some such harmless-sounding name, that came in pint or quart jars. It was mayonnaise mixed with little specks of sweet pickles. It may still be on the market but I'm afraid to look for it because I might find it. When nobody was home I used to load a thick layer of this stuff on a piece of bread and while I was wolfing it down I'd be fixing another slice. I might eat half a dozen slices before I'd quit because I'd hear somebody coming. Even today, when my lunch doesn't quite satisfy, I like to sneak back in the kitchen and make a sandwich of whole wheat bread with nothing on it but low-fat mayo and sliced tomatoes. An excellent combination of flavors.

—

The summers of 1938 and '39 I worked as a soda jerk in the drugstore. For two reasons. One was that the job paid seventeen and a half cents an hour and that was significant pay to me, at a time when we were selling Jersey milk, delivered, for a dime per quart. I've always wondered how the owners of the drugstore arrived at that amount to pay the help. The only reason I can think of even now is that it made bookkeeping easier. Every time a worker put in two hours he would be credited on the ledger with thirty-five cents of pay, and that got rid of the fraction. Of course twenty cents an hour would have avoided fractions altogether but no drugstore would pay that much for jerking soda when some of their adult customers were working full time in offices for less than a hundred bucks a month.

The other reason I took the job in the drugstore was that I could eat, free of charge, all the ice cream I wanted, so long as I wasn't caught eating it when customers were waiting for service. I had friends working then in the drugstore and they guaranteed me that after I had eaten ice cream three or four times a day for a month, even with chopped nuts and chocolate syrup on top, I would never again want any more of it.

They were wrong. I never got tired of ice cream, with or without chopped nuts and syrup. I ate it and ate it, and I would stop and eat it again right in the middle of this sentence if the doctor hadn't told me I ought not to do it on account of my cholesterol. I liked working in the drugstore. The prettiest girls in town came in there to sit and be admired and drink nickel Cokes. And there was all that free ice cream in addition to that.

⏤

When Hard Times began getting a little softer in our little town, meals at home became a lot better than cornbread and beans. We began eating steak maybe once a week. Notice the term is steak, not steaks. I can't recall ever seeing a T-bone or a sirloin on our mother's table. We bought round steak and cut it up and laid it out on a board and beat it tender with the edge of a plate and fried it in that black skillet. Ate it with mashed potatoes and gravy and green beans and biscuits.

We ate more pork than beef. Pork chops, yes. And for Sunday dinner sometimes, a big fresh pork ham with baked sweet potatoes and hot rolls. My father thought one of the greatest of all meals was built around what he called back bone, which was the tender meat from the hog's loin, the part of the animal where pork chops come from. A lot of calf's liver and onions were fixed in that old skillet, and entire flocks of chickens were fried in it.

I seldom eat anything fried now but back when I thought that was the only civilized way to cook, I ate fried chicken in thirty states, and I've decided that the late Mary Elizabeth Adams fixed the best I've ever tasted. For many years Mary was housekeeper for the woman who's now my partner, my wife. We always thought Mary should have gone into the restaurant business and I still think her chicken would have given Colonel Sanders a double-dog fit. But she was a gentle and shy person and wasn't comfortable with the idea.

⏤

When I was working on this book, my sisters gave me one of

their treasures. I have two sisters, no brothers. My sisters are both older and called me Little Brother until I got six feet tall.

The treasure I received was what they call Mama's Recipe Jar. It's a quart jar our mother used to store recipes. Not a bad system. With the lid on tight, the jar has preserved scraps of paper more than sixty years and her penciled script is still legible. It's a sturdy jar with straight sides, beveled at the corners. I think it originally held store-bought pickles. Not one of us in the family can remember seeing that woman write out a recipe and put it in the jar, but my sisters found it in her things after she died. It sits now on top of one of my bookcases, and sometimes I wonder if her fingerprints on the glass would be retrievable.

You couldn't buy that jar from me even if you wanted it, and yet it doesn't contain the recipes I hoped it would. The meals I remember best and loved the most are not there. When she heard about a tricky dessert or a casserole she hadn't tried she'd record the recipe and stick it in the jar. But she'd never save a recipe for her cornbread, or her biscuits, or her coconut cream pie, or her shoulder roast she fixed for Sunday dinner with potatoes and onions and carrots. We don't have her recipe for chicken and dumplings, either. Those and a hundred other dishes were in her head and she didn't need to record the directions. That's a problem many families have run into. They spend their lives at the table of a loving cook and one day she dies and nobody has asked her how she fixed the meals they enjoyed the most.

Another little problem is that some of your best cooks can't really tell you how they cook. I didn't realize this until I was sixty years old and suddenly found myself living in that bachelor apartment. I was acquainted then with a few women I knew were excellent cooks because I'd eaten in their homes.

I'd call them and ask how to fix green beans, or carrots, or pasta, and my questions were so simple and basic that I'd get no satisfactory answers. If I asked how much salt to add they'd say, "Oh, I don't know. Not too much." Lot of help that was.

Which reminds me of Uncle Luby Morrow's recipe for chicken and dumplings. I think this recipe was in one of my previous books but I want to use it here because it fits. I never met Uncle Luby. He lived in East Texas, at Longview. I got the recipe from his niece, Opal Pearson of Houston. It's my favorite of all the recipes I ever heard or read, even though you can't really follow it and cook anything. Never mind that. It's still a great recipe. Ms. Pearson gave me it to me as a dialogue she had with Uncle Luby, after she'd asked him how to fix his wonderful chicken and dumplings.

"Take you about a three-pound chicken," Uncle Luby said, "and put it in a big pot. Cover it with water. Put a good tight lid on, and let it simmer till the meat falls off the bone. Then you take some flour and a little salt . . . "

"How much flour?" Opal Pearson asked.

"Oh, for a chicken that size I'd say a good cupful. Then put you in some shortening and mix it up real good and . . . "

"How much shortening?"

"Well, not as much as if you was makin' a pie crust."

"A tablespoon?"

"A big tablespoon. But don't use no bakin' powders. That's a mistake a lot of people make, is puttin' bakin' powders in dumplin's. Then you put you in an egg and some milk and work you up a good smooth dough . . . "

"How much milk?"

"Well, not as much as what you got egg."

"Half an eggshell full?"

"Yeah, the big half. Then you roll your dough out paper thin, cut it in strips, and drop it in your broth which is at a rollin' boil. Keep forkin' the dumplin's down and separatin' 'em or they'll stick together. Let 'em boil at high speed …"

"About how long?"

"A right smart while. Then you turn your fire down to simmer, put the lid on tight, and don't let nobody take that lid off until them dumplin's are done."

"How long do you cook them with the lid on?"

"Well, not quite as long as you did with the lid off. And that's all there are to it."

Opal Pearson told me this recipe works well for those who know what a good cupful and a big tablespoon are, and how long a right smart while is. Also remember not to use no bakin' powders.

In Mama's Recipe Jar we found the directions for making a fruit cake that became a holiday specialty of my sister Maifred. She wasn't fond of citron and some of the other candied fruits traditional in this kind of cake. So she left them out and devised this sort of simple fruit cake that I loved, and still would if she'd ever make one again. I've always thought of it as Maifred's Simplified Fruitcake. The only fruits in it are dates, pineapples and cherries, which is plenty of fruit if you ask me.

In the last fifty years I've sampled fruitcakes made by scores of women and even a couple of men and I can't remember ever eating a bad one. One time when I was ranging around Texas getting fuel for my newspaper column I did a story on one Gladys Farek who made fruitcakes at her home a few miles outside the little town of Flatonia. She made great lots of these cakes for sale, and blended the batter in a concrete mixer. I have pictures to prove it, or I once did.

Later on she sent me a fruit cake in the shape of Texas and I swear it was three feet wide. I gave it up for auction at a charity event and it sold for a good deal of money. I don't remember how much but I remember it was a tasty cake despite all the geography it covered. I was given a slice of the western edge that enabled me to consume the entire city of El Paso at one bite.

In the middle to late 1930s, at least in the part of the world we lived in, fruit cakes enjoyed high popularity. They were a luxury. A family who could spend money on a fruit cake was on a financial climb. People talked a lot about fruitcakes, especially around Christmas, in the same way they talked about decorating the house and cooking a turkey. These were the same people who strung electric lights not just on their Christmas trees but also on their shrubs in the front yard.

We heard stories about fruitcakes that were many years old, and still good because they were wrapped in cloth and moistened with wine, or brandy. I don't believe my family ever had outside Christmas lights but we did have fruitcakes that lasted a long time. Sister Maifred would make one of her cakes early, before Thanksgiving, and it was stored in the pantry in a tin container and wrapped in a cotton cloth moistened with wine. I bet that wine for the fruitcake was the only alcoholic beverage ever to enter our house as long as my mother was alive. When nobody else was at home I'd take my friend Dude in the kitchen and show him where the bottle of wine was kept. We didn't touch it, though. Our mother preached frequently about the evils of alcohol and by the time I was fifteen I supposed that if I swallowed a mouthful of wine I'd go straight to hell. Yet she allowed wine in the house for fruit cakes.

On special days she took the cake down and unwrapped it with great care. Peeled away the cloth slowly, as doctors do in movies when they're taking the bandages off after eye surgery and we're about to find out whether the patient will be able to see anything. The cake looked dark, almost black. She'd slice a few thin pieces and give us all a taste and we'd talk about how wonderful it was and then she'd wrap it again and put it away. I don't remember ever seeing her pour wine on the cloth and I've always suspected she did that in private, so her children wouldn't have to see their mother handling spirits. But I haven't forgotten the wonderful rich nutty aroma that escaped from the tin when it came open, after being shut up for weeks.

Uncle Barney Hale, our father's younger brother, ate with us one Christmas during the fruit cake time. Uncle Barney was a sort of renegade brother who gambled and didn't mind taking a little drink now and then, or even daily. Sister Ima Ruthie and I loved him dearly and celebrated when he came to see us and grieved when he left. Our Methodist mother didn't approve of his habits but he was good about abstaining when he was in her house. I know she loved him and prayed every night that he would see the light and change his wicked ways.

After that Christmas dinner she brought out the tin and opened it and unwrapped the fruit cake and the rich winy aroma rose up. She cut the little slices and said, "Barney, do you want a piece of this fruit cake?"

He answered, "No, but I'd sure like to suck that rag."

When I began this book I asked my sisters to recall one meal typical of what we ate in the late thirties when we were recovering from the Depression. We had escaped from cornbread and beans and turnip greens and gone on to this, which sister Maifred remembers:

Chicken fried steak, with cream gravy and mashed potatoes. (Cream gravy is what I've been calling skillet gravy.) Then a salad of head lettuce chopped fine and tomatoes, with a dressing of homemade mayonnaise. "You made the mayonnaise with Wesson oil," my sister says, "and egg and lemon juice and salt and white pepper. Made it in a small crock jar with straight sides and a rounded inside bottom that just fit the hand-operated rotary egg beater, and the oil was added in drops between beats."

Then here's another meal my sister Ima Ruthie remembers:

Meatloaf. Fresh green beans and new potatoes. Corn on the cob. A salad of some kind. Hot rolls with butter. Iced tea. And pie or cake, sometimes with homemade ice cream.

Ima Ruthie, two years older than I, was often involved in the preparation of such a meal, which would be a Sunday dinner, meaning we ate it around one o'clock, after church.

"On Saturday morning she would snap the green beans and peel the new potatoes and boil them together with a piece of salt pork." That's Ima Ruthie, telling about the fixing. "When the potatoes cooled they stayed in the ice box until they were warmed up after church Sunday. The corn was shucked and washed on Saturday, and boiled on Sunday morning. Most times she fixed the meatloaf on Saturday but it was never cooked until Sunday. She baked the pies and cakes on Saturday, too."

It's interesting to me that both these sisters, speaking of

food prepared by their mother, never refer to a refrigerator. They always say ice box, because they first watched these meals being prepared in a kitchen that had no electric refrigerator. The ice box was brown, and wooden, and would hold a fifty-pound block brought in the house by the ice man. A shallow pan in the bottom caught the melt. One of my earliest chores was to carry the pan out and dump the water on the violets and nasturtiums. We got our first electric refrigerator when I was in junior high. I remember the payments on it were $5 a month.

Ima Ruthie, still talking: "Mama never threw any food away. She gave plenty of it away—mostly to beggars or bums who came to the back door. What she didn't give away she kept to make a stew-like mixture she called What-Have-You, made up of bits of leftover chicken or pork and covered dishes of vegetables out of the ice box. We'd have this on wash day with yellow cornbread cooked in the old iron skillet, and big goblets of cold buttermilk.

"For her meatloaf she wouldn't buy pre-packaged or pre-ground meat. She ordered it ground fresh—one pound of beef mixed with half a pound of pork—, and she preferred to watch it being ground. Once in a while she'd send me after the meat and I always hated to ask the butcher to go to all that trouble but Mama would say, 'That meat order sometimes runs at least a dollar so he shouldn't complain.'"

—

When I grew up I went to college, which was a surprise to me. I always supposed I would stay where I went to high school and maybe get a job at the power plant that provided our town's foremost payroll. But instead I ended up in Lubbock where Texas Tech University is, and I enrolled there and studied journalism. Probably this was the greatest thing that ever happened to me because I can't now think of what they might have paid me to do at the power plant, other than mow the grass.

My sophomore year at that school I moved into a new dormitory where room and board cost $25 a month, while my sisters stayed home and worked and sent that money for me to eat and sleep. I have never paid them back and won't ever be able to. Sister Maifred, ten years older than I, attended TCU for two years but had to drop out to help feed the family, and Ima Ruthie never left Eastland for college or any other reason. She's still there. This was a time when families often said, "Our sons must be educated but our daughters can get married and have babies or become secretaries." Which was a lot of sexist baloney but it was then a common view.

I lived three years in that dormitory at Tech and those were happy times. Part of the reason was the food. Most of the guys bitched about it, the way institutional food always gets bitched about, but it was wonderful food and so inexpensive. I'm talking about chicken fried steak and beef stew and pork chops and huge deep-dish casseroles containing chicken and peas and celery and carrots. Desserts of cherry pie and ice cream and banana pudding and chocolate cake. I still don't understand how that sort of food was provided for the money we paid.

The waiters in that dormitory dining room were students but they were in no way considered to be in servile circumstances. Most were juniors and seniors and some were big men on campus. They earned their room and board for being waiters and those were not jobs. They were positions, and hard to come by. I wanted in the worst way to be a waiter in that dining room. I applied when I was a sophomore but I was never chosen.

While I was at college I got hooked on Mexican food, not in the dorm dining room but in cheap restaurants. Before Lubbock I'd never eaten Mexican food other than chili and tamales. My mother didn't cook anything in this style, unless it was Spanish rice, but my father often brought home hot tamales and chili. Sometimes the chili would be in cardboard containers carried by thin wire handles. Or it might be what we called brick chili, cooked and molded in butcher shops, to be brought home and heated. But in my early experience, we didn't go out and eat Mexican food in restaurants. Tamales and chili were on my family's table so often I didn't consider them Mexican. They were just plain every-day food. Some of the restaurants in our town served chili but it was considered to be in the same class as pinto beans. Low grade fare, that is.

I remember one scene in a café on the Eastland County courthouse square. A hungry-looking fellow walked in off U.S. Highway 80 and ordered a bowl of chili. Understand this was a good-sized bowl, and along with it you got lots and lots of crackers.

The fellow began by eating about half the chili, straight, while nibbling a couple of crackers. Then he reached for a double handful of crackers and crushed them and dropped the crushings in the chili until the bowl was full again. He stirred, and ate about half that chili and cracker mixture. Then he took a bottle of ketchup and turned it up and beat it on the bottom until it gave down most of its content. Café managers understood this process and always put a lot of vinegar in their ketchup bottles, so what came out was like thick tomato soup. The guy added more crunched crackers until his bowl was almost full again. He shook in some green pepper sauce that was on the counter. Stirred again and ate his mixture of ketchup, crackers and pepper sauce. Drank a big glass of water, pitched a dime on the counter and walked out patting his stomach.

In Lubbock the restaurant people were more particular about guarding their ketchup bottles, and their crackers, as well, so I never managed to work that bowl of chili scam, and I never was that hungry, anyway. But I remember some really outstanding bargains. On College Avenue the tailor shops were in a price war and you could get a pair of pants cleaned and pressed for nine cents. And you could go to a café and get a plate of enchiladas for half a dollar and doctor them with hot sauce until your tongue blistered. This is where my affair with Mexican food began and it's still flaming.

# West Texas Fried Pies

I asked my sister Ima Ruthie about Mama's pie recipe and she did a little research. Here's what she came up with:

*The most popular fruits used in fried pies are apples, peaches and apricots. Usually they are dried or frozen, but canned or fresh can be used. The fruits are stewed in water, drained, and sugar added to taste. Spices such as cinnamon may be added, as desired.*

*One friend's mother omitted the fruit altogether, just adding cinnamon, sugar and butter to the crust, folding it and deep frying to a crispy golden brown.*

*A variety of crusts have been used over the years. Our mother used biscuit dough, thinly rolled. One experienced cook I know said that her crust was "a little bit shorter than biscuit dough, but not quite as short as regular pie crust.*

*The following recipe makes a tasty pie when deep fried, or when baked on a buttered cookie sheet if the pies are brushed with butter before and after they come out of the oven.*

*Filling:*
*3-4 cups of stewed fruit: apples, peaches or apricots; add*
   *sugar, butter, spices to taste*
*Crust:*
*2½ cups flour*
*¾ tsp. salt*
*½ tsp. baking powder*
*1 T. sugar*
*Sift these ingredients together and cut in:*
*½ cup Crisco*

*Mix together and add to other ingredients:*
*1 egg*
*4 oz. evaporated milk*
*Stir together until dough comes into a ball, knead lightly,*
  *fold, and pat out to flatten.*
*(Makes approximately eighteen saucer sized pies.)*

Normally crusts are cut around an inverted saucer, but some cooks just roll a ball of dough into a flat circle. The pies can be any size, but our mother's pies were about the shape of a woman's hand.

The method is this: Take a tablespoon or two of fruit and place slightly off center on the circular crust, then fold the long side of the crust over the filling so the edges match, sealing them together by pressing with a fork. Then deep fry them in oil. One of my friends uses peanut oil, very tasty!

A seventy-seven year old friend recently expressed her love of fried pies as a child. She added that she hadn't eaten one in years, but she didn't imagine today's pies "tasting right," since "no one these days would fry them in that good old hog lard!"

## Mary Elizabeth Adams' Fried Chicken

Mary Adams cooked her chicken for me one day while I took notes. This recipe is taken from that session. The comments are Mary's, as she cooked.

*Corn oil*
*A roll of absorbent paper towels*
*Six drumsticks and six thighs of a medium-sized fresh*
*    chicken; free-range, organic is excellent; or a top quality*
*    supermarket variety, and it's best if never frozen. If you*
*    use chicken breast, decrease the cooking time slightly;*
*Aluminum foil*
*Salt*
*Cayenne pepper, finely ground*
*Plastic wrap*
*Clean paper sack, or plastic freezer bag*

*Wipe the chicken pieces with a damp paper towel. Don't wash; "Water takes the flavor out."*
*Lay the pieces out on aluminum foil or paper towels and season lightly with salt and cayenne pepper. Be careful to sprinkle the seasonings "sparingly. You don't have to cover the whole chicken with it."*
*Using tongs or fingers, put the chicken in a glass dish, cover with plastic wrap and refrigerate overnight.*
*In a ten-or twelve-inch iron skillet, heat enough corn oil to cover the chicken pieces half-way; heat to 350 degrees*

*(medium hot). It's ready when the oil is bubbling modestly and a drop of water flicked into the skillet goes "pop."*

*While oil is heating, put "two cooking spoons" (or half a cup) of flour into a clean paper sack or plastic freezer bag and add the chicken, shaking until chicken is coated.*

*When the oil is hot, remove chicken from sack, shaking off excess flour, and place several pieces into the skillet, skin side down. Don't crowd them. In a ten-inch skillet, fry only six thighs or drumsticks at a time, turning to brown evenly on all sides.*

*Cut the heat down to 300 degrees (medium) and cover the skillet.*

*Cook for fifteen or twenty minutes, then turn the pieces. Again, use tongs, not a fork. Piercing the chicken "lets the flavor out."*

*Cover and cook for an additional ten or so minutes.*

*Place the cooked chicken on paper towels to drain.*

*Feeds 4-6*

## Maifred's Simplified Fruit Cake

½ cup shortening
1 cup sugar
2 eggs
½ cup grape juice
1 T. lemon juice
1 tsp. vanilla
2¼ cup flour
¼ tsp. salt
½ tsp. soda
1 tsp. cinnamon
½ tsp. cloves
½ tsp. nutmeg
½ cup chopped dates
1 cup candied pineapple
1 cup mixed candied cherries
1 cup chopped nuts

*Cream sugar and shortening together, add eggs, and beat until well mixed.*

*Sift dry ingredients together, use part for dredging fruit.*

*Combine all ingredients in cake or loaf pan, adding dredged fruit last.*

*Bake at 300 degrees about 3 hours, placing pan of water in bottom of oven.*

*Proportions may be doubled for larger cake.*

## Mama's Meatloaf

My sister Ima Ruthie says our mother always felt that putting milk rather than eggs in a meatloaf made it more moist and tender.

*1 lb. ground beef*
*½ pound ground pork*
*1 small green pepper, chopped*
*1 small onion, chopped*
*2 slices white bread torn in small bits*
*Salt and pepper to taste*
*Milk*

*Mix all ingredients and pour in enough milk to moisten and make ingredients stick together.*
*Shape into a loaf and place in greased roasting pan or baking dish.*
*Pour one can of tomatoes over top.*
*Bake 1 hour and 15 minutes at 350 degrees.*

# In the Army Now

*T*he first meal I ate courtesy of the U.S. Army was at Sheppard Field at Wichita Falls, Texas, when I'd been a buck private for less than twenty-four hours. The main dish—the only dish, now I think about it—was GI stew. You could find a little beef in it and it had a lot of husky carrots and potatoes cooked to destruction and scattered corn and something that was once green but I couldn't identify it. I thought this stew wouldn't have been bad if they'd heated it up a little more, and maybe put in some pepper. I noticed my fellow buck privates were looking at their trays and lifting their upper lips and wrinkling their noses. The drill instructor who'd brought us through the front gate and into military life made an announcement: "You better get used to this. You're gonna be eating it until the war's over."

From that day the war needed three years to get over with and I suppose I ate GI stew a thousand times and ended up liking it pretty well. In fact, I never really had much trouble with military mess hall chow. The men bitched constantly about it, the same way they bitched about the food in the dormitories at school. They also bitched about the length of chow lines. They bitched about the barracks being too cold, or too hot. They bitched about having to rise at 5 A.M. and dress and fall out and line up for roll call. They bitched about everything. When they couldn't think of anything else to bitch about they went back to GI chow and bitched about that again.

But I stayed healthy on Army chow, and gained weight. Within six months I was weighing 160 pounds for the first time ever. I remember writing letters home about that and telling everybody military life agreed with me and if I could just keep from getting killed in the war I might stay in the Army and become a career soldier. But I changed my mind about that after I got overseas where the shooting was going on.

After I did get over there, a good many of the experiences I now remember had little to do with the fighting.

I remember the weather in Italy on one particular day. It made you want to stay inside. A damp wind whipped the tents of the 415th Squadron, 98th Bomb Group, 15th Air Force. February of '45. I was cold. We'd been in the sunny Italian boot almost a year and I couldn't remember ever being really warm.

Six of us, all members of the same B-24 crew, were hunkered down around the smoky little stove in our tent. Having a bull session. We were unmarried hetereosexual males in our early twenties so you might guess we were talking about girls.

No. The subject was chow. We were each making up the

menu of the meal we'd eat if we could have anything we wanted. In that cold tent we often talked about food.

That morning we had rolled out of the blankets at four o'clock to eat a GI breakfast and attend briefing. We waddled out to the airplane in that cumbersome World War II flight gear, carrying headphones and parachutes. By sunrise we were waiting in line to take off. The target was a marshalling yards at Vienna, not one of our favorite places to visit because that city bristled with anti-aircraft guns. I had been to Vienna five times already and wasn't much interested in going back. The 15th would send you home after you flew fifty missions, and at this time I had something like forty-five. I was looking for milk runs, easy missions. Not Vienna again.

While our B-24 was standing in line to carry bombs to Vienna that morning, it trembled and shuddered and seemed unsafe, right there on the ground. I hated that airplane. The B-24 was an effective combat aircraft but I counted it one of my enemies. I always had the feeling the thing would explode on the takeoff run before it got airborne. I remember one that decided to flare up and burn while sitting still, its engines silent and nobody near it. I could show you pictures.

I'm telling you this war experience because I want to emphasize that when I climbed into a B-24, I almost always thought of what this book is about—food.

Something I learned by being in a war is that just before men go into combat, they often think of things other than the action to come. The nose gunner in our crew told me he always thought about seven-card stud, the poker game. He had won a lot of money playing this game and he found a comfort in dwelling on it before we took off. He saw himself catching the right card on the last round and filling a straight and winning a month's pay from somebody he didn't like.

We had a waist gunner who was in love with a pretty girl back in San Francisco. I saw her picture so many times I could have picked her out in a crowd. Before we took off on a mission that gunner lay back in the waist of the bomber and undressed his sweetie and made love to her. A lot of that kind of thing went on among guys in combat. You thought about whatever gave you comfort.

I wasn't in love then, or at least not much. I didn't have anybody waiting for me at home as the waist gunner did. I'm a terrible poker player so I found no satisfaction in visualizing a stud game the way the nose gunner did.

My comforting thought was about things to eat. I was always cold when we were loaded up and ready to fly off to the war. I'd be shivery even on warm mornings, so I would think about a hot meal from home, with everything I loved to eat when I was growing up. Thinking about home cooking helped get me through that war. It soothed the trembly feeling in my stomach, and in my spirit.

That cold morning in '45 we didn't get off the ground. The weather cratered and the mission to Vienna was scrubbed. We taxied back and parked and piled out, all of us in a high humor, jabbering and joking. Few things I can think of now could lift the spirits of our crew quicker than a scrubbed mission. It meant that for at least one day, we didn't have to go up and get shot at. By nine o'clock, instead of flying toward a target in Central Europe, the six of us sat around the little oil stove in the tent and talked about our favorite meals.

The topic had a particular appeal to me because privately I often thought of the last meal I would have. Newspapers used to describe in detail the last meals requested by convicts facing execution. I always studied those requests with great interest.

In Italy I lived with the romantic notion that I would surely be killed in that war. I had written letters to my family and to a few special friends, saying I loved them, something I wasn't able to say to their faces. I hid the letters in my effects and labeled them, "To be opened only in case of my death."

When we'd fly north over the Adriatic Sea, headed for Munich or Vienna, I would think dark thoughts about catching a chunk of flak in a bad place and my last meal would have been a GI breakfast at 4:30 A.M.—rubbery scrambled eggs, cold toast and bad coffee.

So there in the tent with my buddies, talking about chow, when it came my turn I described what I'd like to have before every mission. What I wanted was my Methodist mother's fried chicken Sunday dinner, the meal we used to have after church when the preacher came to eat with us. Everything was better when the preacher came.

I'm seeing a big platter piled high with fried chicken, probably two whole birds. The pieces have batter on them but it's thin, not the thick grease-soaked gunk you get on chicken at so many fast food places. Then a great bowl of mashed potatoes, creamy and smooth, fixed with butter and milk. You plopped a glob on your plate and flooded it with my favorite kind of gravy. This gravy was made in the great iron skillet and some of the chicken fat was still in the pan. Our mother would brown a little flour in that fat and add milk and stir until the gravy reached the right thickness and it was speckled with pepper and bits of browned chicken skin that came off in the cooking.

I would also want fresh snapped green beans, but not crunchy and half cooked as such beans are served now in restaurants. The ones I remember were limp, in fact, and shiny, and had a flavor I no longer associate with green beans.

Sometimes they were cooked with what we called new potatoes, about the size of golf balls. But with this meal we're reconstructing I'll stay with mashed potatoes because I want to pour that skillet gravy over them.

If for some reason I couldn't have mashed potatoes, I'd want the skillet gravy anyhow and I'd spoon it over biscuits. You took a couple of biscuits and broke them open and laid out the halves on your plate and drowned them with gravy. Put on a little extra pepper, maybe, and get after them with a fork. However, when the preacher came to eat with us I didn't do biscuits and gravy that way because our mother felt it was a countrified style of eating. She was trying to get the country out of us. She did get most of it out of my sisters but a good deal of it stayed in me, and is still there.

The bread I'd like would be our mother's biscuits or rolls and the butter to go on them would be fresh out of the churn on the back porch. I'd really prefer biscuits and rolls and cornbread, all three, but that would be overkill on bread.

For dessert my choice was coconut cream pie. When the preacher came he'd be offered options. "Would you like coconut cream pie, Brother Walker, or blackberry cobbler?" If they'd ever asked me that question, I'd have taken some of both.

So, there you are, the best meal I could think of in the cold tent that day in Italy—fried chicken, mashed potatoes, skillet gravy, green beans, buttered biscuits and a double-header dessert of coconut cream pie and blackberry cobbler. And I can't think of anything I'd rather have today, half a century later.

I once described that meal to a nutritionist, and she shook her head and gave me a sad smile. "It's loaded with saturated fat," she said. "It's not a healthy meal."

True enough. That skillet gravy I loved was made with chicken fat. Bad for my blood vessels and heart. And I've been convinced that those limp, slick, green beans had that exceptional flavor because they were cooked with generous amounts of bacon grease. Pork fat. Saturated fat. Every diet study in the last forty years has told us that consuming excessive amounts of saturated fat is an effective way to clog arteries and cause heart attacks. Even the mashed potatoes were loaded with butter and milk, more saturated fat. And coconut cream pie and blackberry cobbler, with their lard crusts? The nutritionist said she hoped I drank water with that meal because if I did it was the only healthful thing I swallowed. Actually, most times at home I drank milk. Whole rich milk from Jersey cows.

———

The chow served in Army mess halls during World War II would probably have come closer to pleasing that nutritionist, even though very little of it was as flavorful as the food we ate at home.

The main thing I didn't like about GI chow was beets. Beets seemed to follow me everywhere I went in the Army. I had never eaten beets at home because I was suspicious of a vegetable that looked like a purple turnip and yet had no really distinctive flavor.

The main trouble with beets in mess halls was caused by the guys on the serving lines. They were all teed off about being on KP duty and needed others to share their misery. So they would dip into the beets and slop them onto your tray and do their best to get lots of beet juice on your mashed potatoes or your squash or your bread. I always hated that purple look on anything I was supposed to eat.

The other GI food I had trouble with was SOS, which was hash on toast and we were challenged to eat this for breakfast. It had a truly unappetizing look. I will go ahead and tell you that SOS was the soldier's abbreviation for shit on a shingle. Men suffering from boredom invented weird nomenclature for the food they ate and none I now recall will whet your appetite. You may think I've already gone past the borders of decency with SOS. Trust me. Most of the others are worse.

Cold rubbery scrambled eggs for breakfast gave me trouble for a while after my gang got overseas and into the real war. At first my position was that if I had to get on an airplane and fly over enemy territory where people would shoot at me and try to kill me, I at least deserved a decent breakfast before I went forth.

But I soon saw that was a weak attitude. On days when we didn't fly we'd always trudge up to headquarters and check the lines on the big map, showing the gains that Allied ground forces were making, inching across Europe, fighting toward Berlin. Those ground forces were slogging it out, sleeping in fox holes, getting shot at, seeing their buddies die. Man, they'd swap their butts for a breakfast of rubbery scrambled eggs and bad coffee. SOS would be a banquet for them.

My outfit was stationed near Lecce, down in the heel of the Italian boot. In peace time this was an olive-growing area but I don't believe I ever ate an olive in Italy until I returned on vacation in 1985. During that war the most precious food was a fresh egg, and they were rare. The scrambled eggs common for breakfast were powdered and had little resemblance to anything a decent hen ever laid.

There was an early-rising sergeant who came around to wake the crews scheduled for missions. He would sweep the

beam of a powerful flashlight over the bunks and shout
something comforting like, "Drop your cocks and grab your
socks! You're going out to win the war today!"

If he had any trouble getting crews up he'd come back and
yell, "Fresh eggs in the chow hall this morning, cooked the
way you want 'em!" That always brought us out of the blankets. Sometimes he lied, and there were no fresh eggs. But we
couldn't take a chance because most times he was right and
you could hustle up to the mess hall and stand there with
your tray and tell the cook you wanted your eggs over easy, or
sunny side up, just as if you were in a restaurant in your home
town. This was such a treat. We had guys in that outfit who
would volunteer for combat missions if they knew they'd get
fresh eggs for breakfast. I was one of them.

The only other place I ever ate a fresh egg in Italy during
that war was in a whore house. Well, not exactly a whore
house. Little pimps on the streets of Lecce would round up
two or three soldiers and take them to a private home. The
man of the house would sit down with the soldiers and ex-
plain that he had never been a Fascist, that he despised Mus-
solini and favored the Allies to win the war.

Then he would take a certain number of lira from each soldier in return for a meal that his wife served. It always included fresh eggs, which was what we wanted. The price
covered the privilege of dancing with his daughters, who
came smiling forth showing bad teeth and putting scratchy
records on a little hand-cranked phonograph. Their mother
emerged with bottles of really terrible booze that they called
cognac but I had never tasted anything like it before and
haven't since, and I still wonder what it was. I am probably
better off not knowing.

The meal would be all right. The father would open a door

and show you three or four old hens, to prove that you were getting fresh eggs. I don't remember anything about the menu other than the eggs. When you're lonesome for eggs they're always excellent, whether they're cooked right or not. After the meal you could give the old man another handful of lira and take one of his daughters in a back room. Or at least that's what I always heard.

—

On the air base outside Lecce we lived in tents inadequately heated with small oil-burning stoves. At night we were forever cold there in sunny southern Italy, even during what were supposed to be warm months. We tried to keep warm by eating whatever we could find that seemed edible. By 1944 Italy had been stripped of almost everything fit to eat, with the exception of bread. I became convinced Italians could somehow make good bread if there wasn't a cup of flour left in the country.

We had a little Italian friend named Gino who came around and did odd jobs for us. He was maybe twelve and was not allowed on the base but daily he came there anyway. He was a survivor, an entrepreneur. He would carry heating oil for our stove and we'd pay him a few lira. He'd take that and buy flour and whatever else his mother needed to make bread and two days later he'd bring us these beautiful crusty loaves and sell them to us for ten times what we gave him to buy the ingredients.

All the bombers carried K-rations meant to sustain the crews in case they were forced down in places where they couldn't find anything better to eat. K-rations weren't bad. Crew members and maintenance people were forever robbing the packages. Every box of K-rations had a little bar of chocolate in it, or at least it was supposed to. It was hard to find a box of the stuff that hadn't been opened and the chocolate bar taken out.

A K-ration also contained a tin of bully beef and we'd take the tins out and keep them in the tent until Gino brought us a fresh batch of bread. We'd open one of those crusty loaves and sort of hollow it out inside and stuff in a couple of tins of that beef. Somebody in the tent would have a bottle of pepper sauce he'd swiped from the mess hall and we'd add some of that and close up the loaf and heat it on our little stove. Bite into one of those loaves and along with its goodness you'd get a hint of heating oil flavor from the heater. That always reminded me of home, from back in 1931 when everything we ate was cooked on the coal oil stove and tasted a little like kerosene.

For Christmas of 1944 my Methodist mother tried to ship me a devil's food cake. What was left of it reached me in early February of '45 and its remains didn't even resemble a cake, in appearance or taste. But I was pleased to have it because that woman had packed the cake in popcorn. I'm talking about real popped popcorn which she had heard made a good packing material for fragile articles. We threw the cake out but we were all hungry for popcorn so we heated it in mess kits and ate it all.

When I was pulled out of school and put into the Army Air Corps I was enrolled for my last sixteen hours of credit, so after the war I had to go back to Texas Tech for a semester to graduate. For one of my journalism courses I wrote a first-person feature about the best thing I ate when I was over in Italy during the war, and it was a Spam sandwich. My professor thought I was spoofing and my fellow students laughed at the notion that a World War II veteran would eat Spam and like it.

The Spam I know is a spicy pork product. Comes in a can. I still see it on grocery shelves. I always liked Spam. When I was batching in the apartment I'd bring home a can or two along with those Vienna sausages. Spam comes out of the can as a small loaf of meat. I used to slice it and heat it up in the skillet for breakfast, or use it to make a sandwich for lunch.

But during WWII Spam got a lot of bad press. Tons of the stuff must have been shipped overseas to GI mess halls and soldiers were forever bitching about getting Spam all the time, and by 1945 everybody in the U. S. had heard that American fighting men were sick of Spam. I always suspected that these complaints came from guys who were a long way from the shooting. A can of Spam would have been a rare treat to some old boy in a fox hole on a Pacific island. I wonder now how much it was worth on the GI market in Italy. More than once I saw a poker player put up a can of Spam to call a bet when he'd run out of money. Where I was in the European Theater of War, I never heard a soldier utter a critical word about that can of meat.

When our squadron flew a mission, the cook fixed everybody a sandwich to carry along. The sandwich was a masterpiece of simplicity. It consisted of a hunk of Spam between two slices of stale bread. Nothing else. No mayo, no mustard, no lettuce, no pickle, nothing. Every man accepted this sandwich with gratitude, and some would eat it before we ever took off, figuring if they got shot up and had to bail out they'd never get to eat it.

Another reason they ate it early was that when a B-24 got to altitude, say up around 20,000 feet, the temperature in the airplane could get down to minus 25 or 30 degrees and if the sandwich wasn't protected it would be frozen stiff and probably wouldn't thaw out before you got back to base.

I never ate my sandwich early. I treasured it but I didn't want my last meal to be a Spam sandwich, in case we got knocked down. Also because it was such a blessing to have later, on the way home. On a mission day you'd get up around four in the morning, maybe even earlier. If you were going to a tough target like Vienna or Munich you might be worried, or scared, and probably both, so you wouldn't eat much breakfast unless it was a rare morning when the cook had fresh eggs. Some guys couldn't hold down any breakfast at all. And you could be in the air seven or eight hours. By the time you reached the target and dropped bombs and dodged flak and got started back home, it might be well past noon. You'd need a while to realize it but on the way home you'd get hungry. Just ravenous.

I devised a simple trick to keep my sandwich from freezing at altitude. I hid it in my clothes. You always wore long underwear on missions, and on top of the long johns you put on a heated jump suit and over that went everything else you wore, including those bulky sheepskin flight suits. The heated suits worked off the airplane's power system and sometimes they didn't get very warm and you'd freeze your butt off. For that reason some guys refused to wear them and would just put on extra layers of clothing. I always used the jump suit but without the heated socks. I ended up putting on thick socks and my Size 11 GI shoes jammed down into those wool-lined flight boots. I decided if I had to bail out over the Alps and try to walk away from those mountains I didn't want to be down there in all that snow without my shoes.

When we flew out over the Adriatic on the way to the war

and got up to 10,000 feet and went on oxygen, I'd tuck my Spam sandwich inside my clothes, against my ribs, between the long johns and the heated suit. During the mission every now and then some move I made would remind me that the sandwich was riding in there against my side and it was a comfort. Maybe it was the same feeling I'd get back in Glen Rose when I was in second grade and could feel my mother's fried pie warm against my ribs when I was carrying it to school.

Coming home, after we'd dropped the bombs and got back over the Adriatic and let down to 10,000 feet, we'd shuck our oxygen masks and start to grin at each other. Euphoria came to us, gradually. We'd done it again, man. We'd gone up there and done what we were supposed to do while they shot at us and it looked like we'd get back home all right. We might have a few flak holes in the airplane and a minor fuel leak or two and maybe one engine was out and the prop feathered but so what, even a B-goddamn-24 could fly home on three engines and maybe even two, if it was going downhill.

Then when we were still two or three hours from home, it hit us. Intense hunger. I'd take my Spam sandwich out of my suit. After the likelihood of a fighter plane attack was past, I had very little to do on the way home other than ride, so I'd spend as much time as possible eating that sandwich and feeling all warm and relaxed. Best sandwich I've ever had. Nothing but bread and Spam.

After the war when I was back home I told my mother about that sandwich and she said she'd never bought Spam because she thought it was too high.

On the Isle of Capri in 1944 I was introduced to real Italian food. In my growing-up time we had spaghetti and meatballs and sometimes macaroni and cheese but nobody ever suggested to me that these had anything to do with Italy. They were just things we had for supper sometimes.

When our crew got about half through our fifty missions we were sent to Capri to attend what was called rest camp. It lasted just a few days and we didn't really rest there. We fished a little, and drank a lot, and ate too much. They put us up in hotels and we ate dishes called ravioli and lasagna. I would later eat tons of that stuff in Italian restaurants but in '44 I'd never heard of them. I'd never even heard the term pasta then, and today pasta is a staple in our diet at home. (My partner makes the best pasta dish I've ever known. Her recipe follows the last section.)

I keep remembering the dinner my crew and I had on the Isle of Capri. It was given either by the USO or maybe the Red Cross. All combat crews received the same invitation in turn. The dinner was meant to be a morale booster, and it was held in a big house once occupied by some celebrity or other. Lot of wealthy people from all over the planet had big places on Capri, and may still for all I know.

When I say my crew was there, I mean the six enlisted men, non-commissioned officers. The four commissioned officers of our crew were invited another night, I'm certain, when younger and prettier women were on duty as hostesses. That's the way it works in the military. The officers get the best of everything, and enlisted men accept that because they can't do anything about it. The lesson to be taken from this is, anybody about to enter military life should try to become an officer because that's where the gravy is.

The hostesses at our Capri dinner were nice, and sisterly,

and even motherly, and during the meal they encouraged us to talk about home, about our families, and girl friends, and what we hoped to do when the war was over. Everybody was invited to talk, and we did the best we could even though we were uncomfortable and wanted to be back in the bar at the hotel where we could relax.

I believe the belly turret gunner was the one who delivered the memorable line. If I'm wrong I beg his forgiveness, wherever he is. When it was his turn to talk about home and family he refused to speak, and one of the nice ladies said, "Son, you haven't said a word all evening and we wonder why."

He replied, his face serious as sin, "Well, ma'am, I haven't been around ladies in a long time, and in the Army we use ugly words a lot and I'm just afraid to open my mouth tonight for fear I'll fuck up."

That may be my favorite story out of WWII. I've heard other versions of the same story but I prefer to believe that what I heard is the original, and I'm pleased to have been there when it came to pass on the Isle of Capri.

Obviously I didn't get killed in that war. In May of 1945 when the fighting was over in Europe I was in the middle of the Atlantic, coming home on a troop ship. About halfway across I dug out the letters I had written, to be read only in case of my death. They seemed ridiculous to me so I tore them up and fed them to the fish.

We landed at Boston. On the trip home we'd heard truly wonderful stories about how soldiers were welcomed as they returned in victory from overseas. The stories said that great multitudes of cheering citizens would be on the docks, and when we walked down the gang plank beautiful girls would fall into our arms and give us kisses and champagne and maybe even take us home and feed us a banquet and bestow their ultimate favors. What a country.

The first person I met face to face when I walked off was a smiling Red Cross lady who handed me a pint of cold milk. She said that's what most of the soldiers asked for when they got off the ship. She looked a little like my mother so I hugged her and went on. The milk was delicious, and a lot better than champagne, at that. All those beautiful girls who populated the stories didn't show up that day, either.

My experience over the next few months was that the Army did a good job of feeding combat people returning from overseas. I got lucky and was sent out to Santa Ana, California where combat returnees were being processed. The military loves the term process. The processing at Santa Ana included serving the best food I'd ever even seen, much less eaten, in the Army or anywhere else. Huge spreads of meats and fresh vegetables and fancy desserts—like chocolate cake, banana pudding, cherry pies with ice cream—and you could go in the mess hall and eat at any hour. There were no chow lines to sweat and the guys who served you were careful not to get beet juice in your mashed potatoes. They grinned all the time, and nodded. The reason they did was that they were German prisoners of war and ever so thankful to be in California working in mess halls instead of being dead in Europe.

Sometimes at Santa Ana I would go to the chow hall and just sit there, and watch the guys eat all that excellent grub, and I'd think of the missions when I counted a Spam sandwich to be such a treat. There was no duty. Nothing you had to do. You could lay on your butt all day. You could even carry ice cream and cake out of the mess hall and eat it in the barracks. I gained weight. For a while at Santa Ana I liked being in the Army. But all that gentle treatment didn't last long. Two or three weeks, and then you were reassigned and shipped out and things returned to normal.

My journalism training from Texas Tech got me an assignment the summer of '45 to Santa Monica where the Army operated a reception center to process liberated prisoners of war. They were processed even better than the ordinary combat veterans at Santa Ana. They lived in the luxury hotels that lined the Santa Monica beach. I went back to sleeping in a tent but I was privileged to eat with the liberated prisoners and they did eat well. I remember going to the quartermaster and getting new khakis because the ones I'd worn coming home on the ship were getting too tight around the middle.

At the Santa Monica center I worked on the base newspaper and one of my jobs was to interview American soldiers who had recently been liberated. I wrote their stories and sent them to their hometown newspapers. Some of those fellows had been back in this country only two or three days when I talked to them and they were still looking mighty gaunt. Every day for several weeks I listened to how they survived in those Japanese prison camps, and the awful stuff they had to eat in order to live. And I ended up swearing that I would never again complain about a meal I was served. After fifty years I can't say I've stuck to that oath but even now, if I sit down to what seems like a bad meal, I sometimes think of those old boys and how they survived in prison camps by drinking ditch water and eating rotten rice with worms in it.

In November of '45 I was sent back down the California coast to Santa Ana, where the Army's returnee base had been converted to a separation center. All that fancy food and the velvet treatment given the combat veterans only a few months earlier was gone, and we ate GI stew again. But nobody complained because we were there to say goodbye to the Army forever. They gave you a pocketful of money and a small yellow insignia to sew on your blouse. It signified that you had been honorably discharged. We called the insignia the ruptured duck, and considered that it was the highest decoration the military could bestow, representing a rank one grade higher than a five-star general.

When they cut me loose I rode the bus into town and went to a barber shop and got a haircut and a shave and tipped the barber fifty cents. Big spender. I intended to find the fanciest restaurant in Santa Ana and eat a steak the size of a dinner plate and then go to a drugstore and have a banana split for dessert. After that I'd think about what I might do with the rest of my life.

But when I walked out of the barber shop a fellow with slick dark hair was standing by the curb. He had on black pants and a dirty white shirt. He asked where I was headed. I said I was going somewhere and eat. He said, "No, I mean where do you live?" I said Abilene, Texas, where my parents were then. He said, "I'm going to Fort Worth. Leaving in half an hour. Give me fifty bucks for gas and I'll get you to Abilene before sundown tomorrow."

Almost three hundred from my mustering-out pay was left in my pocket. I took about ten seconds to think about it, and gave him the fifty and wondered if I was making a mistake.

He said, "Come on," and walked away fast and I hustled to keep up, thinking he might duck down an alley with my money.

He waved me into the back seat of a '39 Chevy sedan. Looked like it had good tires. I'd learned to look at tires because at that time a lot of cars were rolling on mighty thin rubber. Two other soldiers were in the back seat. One was drunk and nursing a pint of potato whiskey. The driver was called Mitch. A woman was in the front seat close beside him and another soldier was up there with them.

Before we got out of California I learned that Mitch wasn't simply traveling. He was in business. He watched for guys with new ruptured ducks on their blouses. He hung out at barbershops and restaurants because he knew that's where freshly-discharged guys headed when they got out of the Army with all that cash in their pockets.

The woman was riding free so on that trip Mitch had four passengers. Three of the four were going to Fort Worth, 150 miles on east of Abilene. They were paying seventy-five each. Mitch said when he unloaded in Fort Worth he'd get into a motel and sleep about twelve hours and then try to hustle up a load of guys going back west. That was his game, driving that Chevy back and forth between Texas and California, carrying discharged soldiers home. He was a good driver.

We left Santa Ana about three in the afternoon and except when we bought gas and fast food, the wheels on that car didn't stop turning until we got into Abilene the next evening around seven o'clock. Mitch didn't believe in stopping to sleep, when he had a payload like that. Somewhere in Arizona we had hamburgers. Mitch said it was the worst burger he could remember. I thought mine was excellent, my first meal as a civilian. At sunrise we stopped again at a little cafe in what must have been New Mexico. I had another hamburger.

Mitch let me out at the T&P Depot and I was glad to be separated from that bunch. The drunk guy sitting beside me had been stinking for the last five hundred miles.

My folks didn't know I was coming. In those times you didn't pick up a phone as we do now and say, "Hey, I'm in California and I'll be home before dark tomorrow." At the depot I called them and there was a lot of whooping and hollering and they came to take me home and we had a great celebration. Celebrating at our house didn't mean breaking out the booze. Celebration meant hugging and talking and laughing and eating.

When we'd got most of the hugging done my mother asked, "Have you had supper?" This was around eight o'clock, and I knew my folks had eaten two hours earlier. I told her that in the last two days the main meals I'd had were two hamburgers and she said, "My Lord. What would you like to eat?"

I went ahead and told her, because I knew she wouldn't sleep before I was fed. I told her about gathering with my crew members in Italy that time, around the oil stove in Italy, to talk about our favorite meals and mine was her fried chicken with green beans fixed in bacon grease and mashed potatoes with skillet gravy.

And that's what I got, that first night at home. They had to go out and get the stuff and I wanted to object but I knew objection was useless. So I had a delicious shower and found a shirt and a pair of pants that still fit, or came close. And at eleven o'clock when my parents would normally have been in bed, they sat grinning at the kitchen table and watched me eat. When I couldn't take another bite my mother gathered up what I left and said tomorrow she would fix a banana pudding.

That was in November of '45. The next January I returned to Texas Tech to finish my last few semester hours toward a degree in journalism. I moved back into the dormitory, and lived with all those kids who'd been seniors in high school when I went in the Army. Now they were juniors and seniors in college, and at meal time all they did was bitch about how bad the food was.

## Old Style Green Beans and New Potatoes

*1 pound string beans or Kentucky Wonders*
*6 or 8 new potatoes (no more than an inch to an*
    *inch-and-a-half in diameter)*
*1 piece salt pork, 2-3 inches square*
*1 large pot, filled three-quarters full with water*
*3 or 4 whole black peppercorns*

*Peel the potatoes.*
*Cut off the stem ends of the beans, then pop the beans in half, stringing them, if needed.*
*Take a sharp knife and score the salt pork deeply in several places. Or you can chop it into pieces about an inch by a half inch in size. Place the pork and the potatoes into the pot.*
*Bring the water in the pot to a rolling boil and add the beans.Reduce the heat to a simmer and partially cover.*
*Cook the beans like this until they are thoroughly done and the potatoes are tender. (Might take a half hour, more or less.)\**
*Season to taste with salt and pepper and an optional pat of butter, and serve.*

*\*At this point, some people will heat a scant tablespoon of bacon grease in a skillet until it is sizzling, then add the cooked beans and potatoes, tossing them lightly in the grease for a few seconds until they are shiny. (You want just enough grease to coat the beans lightly with nothing left over.) Then add salt and pepper if needed, and serve.*

# The
# Family Table

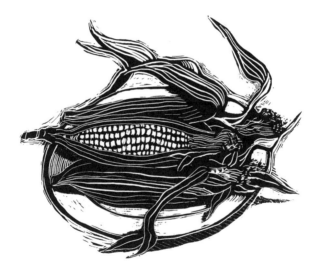

*I* needed seven years to get a college diploma but it did help me find a job at Texas A&M in College Station. I was a sort of press agent there, and for a year I came close to starving. My salary was $200 a month and by the time they finished carving deductions out of it I had about $160 to put in the bank. I was paying thirty dollars to rent a room and eating out every meal and buying a used car and trying to chase girls and the pay check was a joke.

There were days when I thought about the Army again. When I came out as a tech sergeant I was making twice as much as the A&M job paid and maybe three times, considering that I got free room and board and medical care and clothing. But I was convinced in those days that we'd be having another war in a few years, this time with Russia, and I'd had enough of war.

That A&M job taught me how to eat cheap. I found boarding houses where you could get a decent breakfast for thirty-five cents, and a country-style supper of black-eyed peas and biscuits and maybe a pork chop for a buck. But the greatest discovery I made was at the New York Café in downtown Bryan—a plate of three beef enchiladas for ninety cents. Not what you'd call a balanced meal but I ate those enchiladas for supper at least three times a week and never got tired of them.

They were served in the iron plate they were cooked in and when they came out of the kitchen the juice of the meat would be bubbling all around their edges and they were covered in a thick layer of cheese, the kind that would stretch into long strings when you lifted it with your fork. Pierce that cheese covering and lovely little streams of steam spurted out and you had to wait a while before you took the first bite or you'd blister your mouth.

The combination of flavors in a bite of those enchiladas—mainly beef, cheese, onion, tortilla, and cumin—became for me one of the most delicious of all tastes. On pay day I used to head for the New York Café and eat two plates of those babies and sleep like logs.

One night I was sitting at the café counter polishing off an enchilada plate and I felt somebody watching me. He was two stools down, a fellow of maybe sixty with a kind of gray complexion, watching my every bite. I looked back at him, so he could speak to me if I was violating any manners that offended him. He grinned and said, "I was just watching you eat because I would give $500 if I could have a plate of those enchiladas." Meaning that the condition of his stomach wouldn't allow him to eat spicy chow.

Sometimes now, so many years later, when I see young people devouring great plates of Tex Mex food I think about that fellow with the bad stomach and I understand how he felt. Today I have to limit my own intake of Mexican food but it's not because of a bad stomach. It's because of all that cheese and grease that the doctor tells me I mustn't eat.

The New York Café was operated by a big broad Greek named John Miniatis. When he retired and the cafe closed I went into grief, and then began a search for enchiladas as good as those I lived on so long, for less than a dollar a plate. I've never found them. Over forty years, in my travels over Texas, I tested enchiladas in scores of Mexican restaurants, searching for the flavor I remember from the New York Café. Sometimes they came close. John Miniatis' enchiladas ranked ten on my scale, and I found others I graded as high as eight and I had evenings of weak judgment when I gave out a couple of nines. Probably I shouldn't have.

Tex Mex food has been a big thing in my life, almost as big as my mother's fried chicken Sunday dinner. I still eat it once a week, at a place that prepares a few Mexican dishes in health food style. I have an idea what John Miniatis would think about such dishes, that don't even involve rat trap cheese or hot grease.

I've eaten so much Tex Mex that I've developed a sort of possessive attitude toward it. I do a lot of complaining about restaurants that do a bad job of preparation, and serve food that has no more flavor than Johnson grass hay. Nobody pays me any attention, though.

The worst thing about contemporary Tex Mex is that it's cold before you can eat it, and I think that's because it's not hot enough when it comes out. When I first acquired enough money to go in a Mexican restaurant and eat enchiladas, I'd often send them back to the kitchen to be heated, even when the plate was priced at no more than a buck and a half.

In the 1960s I invented a system that Mexican restaurants could use to keep their food hot while the customers ate.

Well, I didn't actually invent it but I did have the idea and what's more important? Nothing was ever invented unless somebody dreamed up the idea to begin with.

Under my system restaurants would have these wired tables, with terminals running to each diner's position to connect with a sort of hot plate. An order of food meant to be hot, such as enchiladas, would be placed on the hot plate to stay heated throughout the meal. You'd have a rheostat control beside your plate and if your food got too hot you could reduce the current, and you could heat everything up if it threatened to get cold.

Aren't you tired of ordering hot food, and eating half of it cold? Not just in Mexican cafés. Most kinds of restaurants could use this improvement. Italian places, especially. You get a beautiful bowl of hot pasta and take four bites and listen to the person on your right tell about what his dog did yesterday and when you go back to your food it's cold paste.

I believe this is why so many diners walk out of Italian restaurants with half their dinner in a plastic container. They're taking it home to heat it up.

—

A few years ago I mentioned those New York Café enchiladas in the column and I got a letter from Phyllis and Jim Miniatis who live in San Antonio.

Jim is John Miniatis' son, and worked in his father's restaurant when he was a high school boy. We corresponded and established the high likelihood that Jim served me a few plates of those enchiladas when I was living on them back in '46. He and Phyllis invited me to spend a night in their home, and Jim would make enchiladas exactly like those perfect ones I remembered, and I could have some Number Ten 'ladas at last.

So I went to San Antonio for the Great Test. We had a couple of cold ones and talked about the old days and then all went to the kitchen for the preparation of the enchiladas. Phyllis had all the ingredients laid out beautifully. The ground beef and the shredded cheese and the onions and the corn tortillas. Jim rolled and cooked the enchiladas in the very same iron pans used in the New York Café when I was eating there.

They were, of course, delicious and I gave them a 9.7. I wanted desperately to give them a 10, since Jim and Phyllis had opened their home to me and gone to all that trouble, but I just couldn't do it in good conscience. They were the best enchiladas I'd had since the 1940s and yet, some vague element was missing. I couldn't quite detect the exact flavor and the texture that I remembered and expected.

Driving home I decided why Jim's enchiladas were not 10's. It was because 10's don't exist, or at least they exist only in my memory. For forty years I'd been searching for something that was not possible to find. That trip to San Antonio convinced me that it's probably folly to roam around in search of any food that tastes the way you remember it from decades ago. I had to confess to myself that even my mother's fried chicken, that she'd cooked that first night I was home from the Army, wasn't quite as good as I expected. I still classed that meal the best I ever had because of the circumstances but the chicken, well, it wasn't exactly what my tongue remembered back in the tent in Italy when we talked about favorite meals. In the years I'd been away, I'd thought about that chicken dinner so many times I'd remembered it being better than it was, and I'd done the same thing with those enchiladas, too.

―

While I was working at Texas A&M I met a secretary named Mary Helen Vick. She had never been in the New York Café so I took her in there and she loved the enchiladas the same as I did.

Her mother was Emmie Pipkin Vick, known to her grandchildren as Mimi (pronounced Mimmy), and to most of her large family and friends as Little Emmie. She wasn't quite five feet tall but she became a towering figure in my life and eventually I came to love her as I did my own mother.

Mimi and her husband Clarence lived in a big white frame house on College Avenue in Bryan. After I had the third date with their youngest daughter I was invited into that house for Sunday dinner and almost immediately it was home to me. Within the next year, before Mary Helen and I married, I ate probably fifty meals in Mimi's dining room and after the second or third one I quit feeling like a guest. Sometimes I would just show up, even when Mary Helen wasn't there, and Mimi would feed me.

I loved that woman's dining room. Her table was rectangular and long and on special Sundays when two or three spare leaves were put in it, I suppose it would seat fourteen people. A large stained glass window in the north wall gave the room a church-like atmosphere. A swinging door led into the roomy kitchen, and through that door came great beef roasts and baked poultry and bowls of fresh vegetables with that old-fashioned flavor and beautiful cakes and pies.

Wild game dishes, as well. Clarence Vick was a stockman who ran cattle on a Navasota River Bottom ranch that was home to a great deal of wildlife. Deer, ducks, doves. Fish from the river. One of the specialties Mimi served in that dining room was squirrel stew, the only squirrel stew I've ever eaten in my life and it was excellent.

I always felt Mimi and her husband made an extraordinary pair. She was a Christian who lived her religion daily, without making those around her uncomfortable about it. Her father was a preacher and she taught Sunday School most of her life. She was a gentle, caring person who did a great deal of good in this world. She may have been the best human being I've ever known.

Her husband went to church with her faithfully and that always surprised me a little. He was a big tough red-headed cowman with a short fuse on his temper and a vocabulary of startling profanity when he became inspired. I was always afraid of him, especially when I was courting his daughter and eating too often in his house.

But I discovered that he had a particular weakness. One spring Saturday he said he wanted me to go with him to the river bottom. This was a surprise since up to that time he hadn't paid me much notice. Even when I was within two weeks of becoming his son-in-law I could sit at that big dining table for Sunday dinner and he wouldn't say anything to me other than pass the peas.

We drove to the river which was about fifteen miles from the house and not a syllable passed between us the whole way. I supposed he intended to show me the ranch, and maybe talk about the life of the family I was about to marry into.

No, what he needed me to do was climb up a big dogwood tree he knew in that river bottom, and saw off a bunch of limbs that had especially nice blooms. Under his direction I cut the limbs and loaded them on the pickup and we drove back to town. Then he gathered the flowered boughs from the truck and held them in his long arms and went in the house and presented them to his wife.

It turned out this was a ritual with that crusty-tempered man, to bring flowers to Mimi when nature provided them out in the country. Later in the year I saw him come in from the river with armloads of bluebells, and grinning like a schoolboy.

He was a master gardener. Down in that river bottom he plowed an acre of ground and fenced it off from the deer and raised enough vegetables to supply several families.

One Sunday we were all gathered in that dining room and it was a special meal because Mr. Vick—I never called him anything else—Mr. Vick had brought in his first batch of roasting ears. I mean two or three bushels of them. We had all participated in the preparing the feast, shucking the corn, killing worms, picking silk, boiling ears.

Among the guests at this annual spring fiesta was a good-humored lady with a formidable appetite for corn. Toward the end of the feast she reached for another ear and Mr. Vick asked how many she'd eaten. She said eight.

And he said, right there before the guests and maybe even the preacher for all I know, "Godalmighty, Mildred, I got a horse can't eat but twelve."

Festive Sunday meals of that kind in the Vick home involved probably a dozen people. They were nothing but junior-grade tea parties compared to the annual Christmas party held at Pippy's house. Pippy was Mrs. J.J. Pipkin, Mimi's mother, Mary Helen's grandmother. She would become the great grandmother of my two children, and lived long enough to know both of them well.

Pippy was a widow by the time I walked onto this scene. She lived in a great old house about halfway between Bryan and College Station. Those two cities have grown together but when Pippy's home was built, Bryan and College Station were five miles apart so the house was originally in the country. I was fascinated by that house. It was mysterious and scary, two stories, with a high-rise cupola on top and high narrow glaring windows and a long tree-lined lane leading up from the road. I thought, Wow, put a dark thunder cloud behind this old house and trigger a few lightning flashes around the cupola and you'd have a perfect setting for a film based on an Agatha Christie murder mystery.

Pippy's husband once operated a dairy on that place. He was also a preacher of the Baptist persuasion. All the Vicks and Pipkins were big Baptists and so in a denominational sense I was an outsider, descended as I am from a long line of Methodists.

The first time Mary Helen took me to that house to meet Pippy, there was a problem out in the barn. The fellow who was supposed to show up and milk Pippy's cow had not shown up, and that old girl was bawling and strutted and uncomfortable. Pippy was upset about the matter so I went to the barn and milked, and brought the bucket in and strained the milk and asked whether it ought to be put in the ice box or left out to clabber. This was a familiar process to me.

After that, I was a hero to Pippy. She had never before entertained a visitor who walked in the house and out the back door to milk a cow. This event probably had a lot to do with Mary Helen and me getting married. I married that entire family, which is not often a good idea but I couldn't help it because I fell in love with their life style.

They had wonderful family rituals, such as what I came to think of as the Christmas Convention. Pippy had eight daughters and sons and they had daughters and sons of their own and at Christmas they would all come together and form a multitude in the old house. I don't want to say how many sat down for dinner but I remember one year the women baked four big turkeys. Three or four tables were placed end to end and reached from the kitchen door through the big dining room and into the living room. Place looked like a Chamber of Commerce banquet hall.

There was no wine, no beer, nothing alcoholic. There were no servants. The women of the family did all the cooking and the cleaning. The children sat near their parents at the long table, not off in a separate place. When all were seated a protracted blessing was said, by whom I'm not sure but probably by Charles Pipkin, Pippy's eldest surviving son. The meal was loud, with constant happy chatter and laughter. It was a splendid scene and I loved it.

But the show was just beginning. A twelve-foot tree stood in the living room and beneath it was a broad loose mound of small gifts, one for each person present. When a name was called, that person came forward to accept the present. Then the gift recipient was required to dance around in a circle while everybody else clapped and sang a little ditty I wish I could remember. When the second person rose to receive a gift, he or she joined the first person in the middle of the room and they danced together. Not ball room-style. Many Baptists at this time were still opposed to couples dancing together. I'm talking here about a sort of foot-sliding trot, with arms hooked together. Soon you had four, six, and then eight people going around in that circle and toward the end of the gift-giving, that old house was literally rocking from all those dancing Baptists and I never saw a crowd have more fun. I was not yet a member of the family but I was under suspicion and there was a present for me under that tree. I took it and danced with the others.

———

The following spring Mary Helen and I were married. We lived mostly on enchiladas from the New York Café when we could get them. When we couldn't we tried to reproduce them at home, sometimes with fair success.

When Mary Helen was pregnant with our son Mark, the family joke was that he would be born blowing smoke rings, from all those enchiladas his mother ate. I will say this: His first public eating experience was in Felix's Mexican Restaurant in Houston where he sat in a high chair and ate chili con queso with his fingers and cried. Cried not because the hot cheese was burning him but because he wanted more than his mother would give him. At home, as soon as he could walk, he went out in the back yard and ate two pods of green cayennes off the pepper plants I had growing back there. They blistered his mouth and he yelled a considerable while but I had to put a wire cage over the plants to keep him from harvesting more of my peppers.

Two years later his sister Becky came along, showing similar tastes. So I will be forever convinced that the diet of an expectant mother influences the food preference of her children. Those two are well up into their forties and when they get together now the first thing they do is go out and buy cheese and cans of peppery tomatoes and make hot cheese dip that will skin a normal person's tongue. Their mother was addicted to this preparation and taught them to make it so that as long as they live they could sit around eating on it and talking about her, and they do.

⁓

Mary Helen and I stayed married for twenty-five years and managed to build a pretty nice home and get just about as deep in debt as anybody else. Our house had three bedrooms and two baths and a fireplace in the den and a barbecue barrel in the back yard. It had a basketball goal beside the driveway and a two-car garage with only one car in it but the other half stayed full of junk so it seemed fully occupied.

The outside of that house looked close to the same as everybody else's but the inside didn't measure up to the neighborhood standard. The reason was that we ate too well. When the neighbors went out and bought new living room furniture and expensive drapes, we'd buy a huge food freezer and an entire steer to put in it.

Since Mary Helen's family was in the cattle business it was close to religion that we ate a lot of beef. Steaks on Friday night. Roast beef on Sunday. Hamburger steaks with brown gravy. Tenderized round for chicken fried steaks. Thick Swiss steak, swimming in brown juice. Beef stew. We had so much beef that even the children began turning up their noses at steaks and we turned to fish and chicken and pork.

When the kids were growing up I had my only cooking experience, until much later on when I was batching in the apartment.

For twenty-five years I fixed my own breakfast before anybody else in the house was awake. I didn't do this out of consideration for the sleepers. I did it because I was always really hungry when I woke up, and felt that if I didn't eat a big breakfast right away I would faint. This feeling came on me in early morning no matter how much I'd eaten the night before. In fact, it seemed to me that the more I ate for supper the hungrier I was when I came awake.

I will say for myself that as a breakfast maker, I was at least fast.

During the sixties and seventies I was writing six columns a week for the *Houston Post* and roving over Texas in constant search of material. For ten of those years I took money for posing as a part-time college teacher at Sam Houston State in Huntsville and daily I was doing a short radio commentary on several small stations. In the middle sixties I also wrote my first book and mowed the grass and took my kids fishing weekly and served as assistant manager of a Little League Baseball team. So I was always in pretty much of a hurry.

I used to get up at five o'clock and toss off a few fingers of orange juice to pop my eyes open. Then I'd plug in the coffee pot and take a quick shower and get dressed, in whatever I intended to wear all day. I'd see my neighbor men, later on at seven o'clock, coming out to pick up the paper and they'd look nice in their robes and striped pajamas and leather house slippers. I never was comfortable going outside in a dressing gown, or whatever they're called. I was always getting such stuff for Christmas, from loved ones who hoped to convert me, but I inherited the notion that a man ought to roll out early and put on his clothes and get on with the day. My father was that way. I can't remember ever seeing him walking around the house early in the morning wearing a robe and house shoes. He got up and bathed and dressed and went.

I liked getting up early and having time on my own for a

couple of hours. Fixing my breakfast has never been a problem for me. I've been married now to three different women and not one of them ever developed the habit of cooking breakfast. A few men friends of mine tell me that their wives rise before dawn and go to the kitchen and cook and call their husbands when breakfast is ready. That's amazing to me, and I wonder if it's true.

## Top Side Toast and Blindfolded Eggs

My breakfast was the same for at least twenty years. Two strips of bacon and two blindfolded eggs and two pieces of toast with jelly or jam, mostly blackberry. I've never much liked toast made in a toaster because I grew up eating toast browned on only one side, in the oven. Put four dabs of butter on a piece of bread, positioned evenly in each quarter of the slice, and leave it under the broiler until it threatens to burn. Then you've got a special kind of toast, dark brown and crisp on the top side but soft on the bottom. Spread your jam or jelly on the top side, but don't cover the four spots of melted butter.

The way I timed my eggs in the skillet, I broke them into medium hot bacon grease and went out in the yard to get the paper. Time I got back to the kitchen the eggs were cooked enough on their bottoms and I could start flipping hot grease on them for the blindfold effect. Then scoop 'em onto a plate and dab some of the grease off with a paper towel.

On a standard work day, before seven o'clock I had read the paper and finished breakfast and was at my typewriter, doing the column, before anybody else in the house was awake. Most such mornings if I had a column idea in advance I could get it done in two hours and sometimes by ten o'clock

I'd be fifty miles down the road, going wherever I needed to go.

Which is astonishing to me because on the day I'm writing this sentence, if I had to fix bacon and eggs it would take me two hours. Or more, since I'd need to go to the store to get eggs which we don't keep in the house now. At least not fresh ones. Sometimes we buy a dozen, use four and the rest spoil.

—

Breakfast is the only thing I cooked inside the house when Mary Helen and I were married, but in the back yard I did a lot of what I called cooking.

Along about that time, in the early fifties, back yard cooking was just getting started, and I think it was a farce and still is. If you could establish the origin of twentieth century outdoor cooking I'd bet the farm and all its improvements you'd discover it was a woman's idea. She was sick of cooking and made a sly suggestion that her husband, being so smart and talented, could probably build a fire in the back yard and cook a piece of meat that would be better than she could fix in her kitchen.

This was an outrageous notion. The American woman gave birth to it at a time when she had just acquired a beautiful kitchen with all manner of gleaming conveniences, including even a machine that washed dirty dishes. And what does she do? She cons her husband into cooking in the back yard.

Furthermore, she brags on everything he fixes out there. This is why so many men think they are great at cooking meat outdoors on a charcoal fire. Their wives have told them again and again, "Honey, this is the best we've ever had," when she could go in the kitchen and fix something better in half an hour.

But why should she bother, when her husband will buy the meat and the charcoal and the starter and build the fire and maybe even mix the sauce? And while he's doing all that work she can enjoy a relaxing bath and come out at sundown looking fresh and pretty and sniffing the smoke and saying, "Honey, I never smelled anything so good in all my life."

What makes this scam work is that the men love it. I still wonder whether prehistoric man not only killed the meat but cooked it, while his mate sat in the mouth of the cave and arranged her hair and talked about how good supper smelled.

I was a satisfied victim of this woman plan. I liked cooking in the yard, and I loved it when anybody bragged on what I cooked. I wonder if it was all that good, but never mind now.

I bought a fifty-two-gallon oil barrel converted into a cooking rig, with a lid that raised up and a metal chimney that gave off charcoal smoke. It had wheels. A moveable cooker.

As the years rolled by I began to notice that Mary Helen was cooking less in the kitchen and I was cooking more in the back yard on my barrel. I didn't mind this. I liked it. I imagined the situation came about because I was such an excellent outdoor chef.

That misconception led me into cooking lots of meat at the same time. Some Saturday nights I would cook enough meat to last us a week. T-bones for supper. Chickens for tomorrow. Pork chops for Tuesday. Beef roast for Thursday. Put it in the fridge, or freeze it, and thaw it out four days later.

During my career in barbecue I created several culinary curiosities, all by accident. The most notable of these was my blackened chicken, which I invented years before blackened redfish was on the menu of any New Orleans restaurant.

This came to pass on a day when I had the grill of my barrel covered in chicken halves. My policy on chickens was to fix six or eight birds at once, since they were very little more trouble than fixing one or two. We had a couple of college boys, relatives, going to school near us and they were far from home and always hungry so it was handy to have cooked meat in the freezer when they came to see us. College boys weren't interested in balanced meals. What they wanted was the Four-B Banquet—beer, barbecue, beans and bread.

So I was tending my barrel when I got a call from the city desk. They needed a quote from a source involved in a breaking story and they couldn't raise the fellow by phone. He lived not far from our house so they asked me to run over there and roust the guy out and get the quote and call it in. The desk said it wouldn't mess up my Saturday much. Might take maybe half an hour.

It took three hours. So when I got back to my chickens they were burned pretty well black, and I figured I'd feed 'em all to the neighborhood dogs. However, then I noticed that the burn wasn't too deep so I tasted a drumstick and a thigh and found that inside they weren't even done. They were simply scorched, on the outside. Nothing to lose, so I gave them a good mopping of sauce and stoked the fire and let them cook another hour, and when they were done I was pleased with the way they looked. That extra sauce covering their dark burntness gave them a unique appearance.

I called our college boys and invited them to test my blackened chicken. They came immediately and ate and said it was fine, that it had a sort of underlying crispy texture they never associated with barbecued chicken. My kids were then like twelve and ten and they too said the chicken was good. I suspect their mother had told them to brag on anything I fixed on the barrel but I was accepting all praise from any source. Later on I made improvements in my blackened chicken. The main refinement came through the advice of my friend the late Joe Dillard, a formidable back yard chef. He had given me a fresh venison ham and recommended I cook it on my barrel. He asked, "How do you apply your sauce?" I told him I mopped it on, with one of those little mops made for the purpose and sold in stores. Joe told me to throw it away. He also said throw away my cooking fork that I was using to turn meat on the grill, and buy a set of serious tongs. "This meat needs lots and lots of sauce. It wants to be immersed in sauce. So what you do is make a large batch of it and every now and then you pick up the venison with your tongs and dip it in the sauce and roll it around in there. You want to keep it soaked in sauce."

He gave me a recipe for the sauce he used but I lost it. No matter. A lot of back yard chefs are mystic and secretive about sauce but I think they're mostly just putting on airs. Go to the supermarket and you'll find a dozen brands of bottled barbecue sauce and they're all just jazzed up tomato juice.

## Mary Helen's Barbecue Sauce

Mary Helen used to make a sauce this way for my barbecued spare ribs: Mix a cup of cider vinegar and a bottle of Worcestershire in the contents of a large can of tomato juice. I'm talking about a thirty-two-ounce can. Sometimes she added garlic powder and always a good deal of salt.

For years I used a version of this sauce on everything I cooked outside. Sometimes I'd double the recipe so I'd have a dish pan of sauce and I could tong up two chicken halves at once and baptize them. I never again used a cooking fork to lift or turn meat on my grill.

———

That old barbecue barrel and I spent so much time together I joked to friends that I was beginning to smell like it. Then I learned that maybe it wasn't a joke. I went for a haircut and Jack the Barber told me, "Your hair smells like a barbecue pit."

I burned the bottom out of that barrel two or three times. I'd go to the hardware store and buy some heavy valley tin, the kind roofers use, and double it and curve it to fit the bottom of the barrel and that tin would last another two years.

We associate outdoor cooking with long summer evenings but I liked barbecuing in winter as well. Put on a couple of sides of young spare ribs when the weather was cold, and my neighbor Sam would smell my smoke and come over with a couple of cans of Pearl and we'd lean against the back of the barrel and warm our butts against it and visit and this was good.

Our neighborhood was a circle. A dozen families of us built houses on what I thought of as a round block. It wasn't exactly round but it wanted to be. It was like a big pie, sliced into lots, and most of the back yards tapered and came together at the same point. So we had what amounted to a huge common back yard, with post oaks for shade and it was like a park.

Some of us were victims of the old saw that good fences make good neighbors and most of the families planned to fence themselves off. Then we came to our senses and recognized that we had the opportunity to enjoy something unique, a private multi-family park, so we scrapped the fence plans. Several batches of neighborhood children grew up playing together in that large common back yard. Someone put a picnic table out in the middle, astraddle the property lines, and it became the neighborhood table and everyone forgot who owned it in the beginning.

Several of us had barbecue barrels, and their smoke on summer evenings sometimes led to unplanned feasts. Say I fired up and put on T-bones. Sam might holler from next door and ask if I had room on the grill for a couple of chickens. He'd bring his birds over and pitch them in and then Bob from the south side of our park would see what was happening and bring hamburger patties for the grill, and his next door neighbor Brady would come, and Cheesy who lived behind us, and Jay from on our north side, and I'd need to pour more charcoal on the fire.

The women would begin emerging, all fresh and pretty in their summer dresses, and they'd bring salads and breads and we'd put it all together out there in the yard and eat and laugh and tell stories and for me it's wonderful now, to remember.

Nobody had uttered a word about having a neighborhood gathering and yet there it was, happening, and maybe that was the best part.

If we'd built fences I doubt I'd have these warm recollections. Later on when the kids got tall and threatened to go to college or get married, some of us did put up fences to hold the dogs we got to replace the departing children. But all of us installed gates in the back and on the sides, so we wouldn't cut one another off.

—

The only thing I ever fixed in the kitchen, other than my breakfast, was a picnic salad I invented and contributed when we had those neighborhood feasts. I called it a layered salad and I don't remember now why I thought it was wonderful but I did. I believe the beginning of it came on a day Mary Helen had one of her terrible sinus headaches. Usually when she was incapacitated that way I'd get a meal together, most times by going out and bringing in hamburgers or pizza. But once I thawed out some cooked meat I had in the freezer and made a simple green salad with iceberg lettuce and tomatoes and it was fairly edible.

Mary Helen made the mistake of saying the salad was good. I know she was simply trying to be agreeable but I was vulnerable then to praise, and wanted more. So I began making additional salads, and much larger ones. When we had company I would go forth and buy three kinds of lettuce, and various other greenery, and try to turn out something that guests would brag on. We didn't have a salad vessel large enough to suit me so I bought one the size of a foot tub.

And so my layered salad was born. I still think it was pretty. The idea came to me because most of the green salads I was eating then were pre-dressed and tossed and just swimming in far too much dressing.

## *Layered Salad*

I decided what the world needed was an attractive green salad that had no dressing at all, and diners could shovel individual servings onto their plates and add whatever they wanted in the way of dressing. If they wanted it tossed they could do the tossing on their plates.

I was in love then with the idea of creating something new and different. I felt that cooks in general weren't spending enough time and thought on their salads so I whomped up one that took me a full hour to make, counting the thorough washing of all the greenery. Before this time it had never struck me that a thing like lettuce needed to be washed before it was eaten, but then in my work I happened to visit a field of lettuce and saw all the pesticides that were sprayed on the plants to control the bugs and diseases. Lettuce needs to be washed, trust me.

I began by arranging a neat layer of iceberg leaves in the bottom of my vessel. Next layer was shredded red cabbage, about half an inch thick. Then a sprinkling of fine-diced cheddar cheese. Then a thick layer of leaf lettuce. Next, an application of crumbled blue cheese. On top of that, a layer of crisp inner romaine lettuce leaves. Then a sprinkling of bacon bits, mixed with small dices of celery. Now repeat the layers until the salad bowl is full, and garnish the top with a generous application of shredded cheddar, plus celery leaves and anchovies arranged in an attractive pattern.

When I first began making it I thought my layered salad was a success. People always said it was pretty. Others would deliver comments like, "Now that's a salad." However, I noticed that nobody ate a lot of it, even though I always provided clean tongs to serve it with, and a nice fat bottle of ranch dressing. Once at a picnic where it was in competition with other salads its layers were hardly disturbed. One lady said, "Well, it's just so pretty nobody wanted to disturb it. It's like a center piece."

After that I stopped making it, and decided it was a salad whose time just hadn't yet arrived. But I wish I'd taken a picture of it, made in a huge clear glass bowl so you could see the layers in there.

If I make a salad now I use only one kind of lettuce—any kind that's not iceberg—and toss it with vinaigrette dressing. We make an easy one—one-third balsamic vinegar to two-thirds extra virgin olive oil. You can add hot mustard or pepper but it really doesn't need them.

—

When I was in my mid-fifties I decided I would soon die of lung cancer if I didn't quit smoking. My chest x-rays said I didn't have cancer but I felt I was about to get it, or that I already did and the x-rays had missed it. Some days I could feel it growing in my lung. I have always been talented at producing the symptoms of dreadful diseases even when I don't have them.

Mary Helen and I were both horrendous smokers. Our house reeked of stale smoke, as I discovered after I quit cigarettes. I was the kind of addict who sometimes had two cigarettes going at once. My clothes had holes burned in them and my fingers were stained with tar.

So one day I quit, cold turkey, and struggled through the difficult withdrawal time that all quitters love to talk about. As a substitute for cigarettes, I ate. I ate all day. Every time I wanted a cigarette, I ate. Mostly sweet stuff. I ate Eskimo pies, peanut patties, Milky Ways and Snickers, Mr. Goodbars, ice cream by the quart. All this in addition to regular meals. I became addicted to a confection called burnt peanuts, which are peanuts covered in hard candy. I bought them in king-sized packages at grocery stores and kept my coat pockets full of these peanuts and crunched on the things constantly, until I began having trouble with my teeth.

After six months I had not gone back to smoking but none of my pants would button because I weighed 192 pounds. This fat-gutted dude was once the skinny soldier who wrote letters home, boasting that he had finally managed to attain a weight of 160 pounds.

A doctor friend, who was still smoking then, told me that carrying 192 pounds was probably more harmful to my health than smoking cigarettes. So I went on a diet to get rid of all that fat, and this took an entire year. Mary Helen went on the diet with me. By that time she had been talking back to the bathroom scales several years, despite that she weighed only 103 pounds when we married.

We quit buying bread and bought Melba toast instead. I stopped frying eggs and learned to poach them. We quit cooking on the barbecue barrel and ate mainly salads and at sundown every day we had one small glass of wine.

It took me a while to learn that Melba toast is really edible. At first I considered that it had absolutely no flavor. It was like eating crisp cardboard. But after you go to bed a couple of weeks with no more to eat for supper than two ounces of meat and a small salad with lemon juice for dressing, and you wake up at 5 A.M. feeling lucky that you didn't die of starvation during the night, a piece of Melba toast is a banquet.

After a dozen bad starts I got pretty good at poaching eggs. A chicken egg is such a marvelous food. Cook it twenty different ways and it'll taste different every time. A properly poached egg doesn't even seem kin to a fried or a scrambled one.

Since I always ate breakfast alone and didn't have to worry about protocol, I'd fix two soft poached eggs and drop them in a cereal bowl and crumble two slices of Melba toast over them. Put on a lot of black pepper and a little bit of salt and stir it all up and eat it with a spoon. And a big cup of coffee, black.

That was not a happy year at our house. But at the end of it I weighed 170 instead of 192 and Mary Helen dropped a lot of weight as well. However, she was simply not able to stop smoking. This would cause her serious health problems and eventually lead to her death.

———

After Pippy died, the great Christmas gatherings at her house stopped, and gradually signs that the Pipkin family had lived on that land disappeared. The barn was torn down. The pastures bought up by real estate developers. The great old house razed. An apartment complex stands now on the site. I don't like to look at it.

Mimi lived well up into her nineties and helped us keep going the custom of large family dinners, sometimes at her house, sometimes at ours, sometimes at the home of her son. As long as she could stand, Mimi stood at her stove and cooked good meals. Most of Mary Helen's recipes came from her. All the best ones, I thought.

The dish I really enjoy remembering is Mimi's ambrosia, which we fixed for those large Christmas dinners. I can say *we* because for twenty years I had a part in it. We'd go together and select the coconuts, shaking them to be sure they contained plenty of milk. At home we'd punch out the eyes and drain and save the milk. Break the nuts with a hammer and work through the tedious job of peeling away the dark brown inner covering of the meat.

Then I'd go off with a big pan of that white meat and spend hours grating coconut with a hand grater. When I took it back to Mimi I'd tell her it was flavored with the blood of my fingers and she'd laugh and say, "That's good." I suppose now if people want fresh grated coconut they grind it up in one of those electric kitchen machines. But I'm still pleased that I skinned my fingers grating coconut for Mimi's ambrosia.

My children were privileged to eat many meals in Mimi's dining room, in that white house on College Avenue in Bryan where I first met the family. They still talk about early Saturday mornings after they'd spent Friday night with her and she'd make pancakes for breakfast. I'd go to pick up my kids and Mimi would be in the kitchen doing pancakes not only for my pair but two or three of her other grandchildren who had spent the night. Her batter was thin, and the pancakes were thin as well and small, not more than three and a half inches in diameter. So they didn't need long to cook. I used to walk into her kitchen and she'd be at the stove with the grandchildren standing in line, holding their plates, waiting for another helping. When I saw that—all those little kids and not a one half as tall as Mimi's four feet eleven—I always thought about the dwarfs in the Snow White story.

Eventually the Vick property was sold to an outfit that would build a big cafeteria there. Possessions and furnishings were of course rescued before the house was turned over to the wrecking contractor. But something was left in there that I wanted, and I stole it. I needed help to do it but I'm not saying who helped me. He was in a sensitive public position at the time, and what he did could have threatened his job. We went to that house one night, after it belonged to somebody else, and took out of the north wall of the dining room the stained glass window that I loved, and we carried it away.

This was surely a high misdemeanor if not a felony.

Probably the statute of limitations on stealing stained glass windows has run out by this time but never mind that. I don't want to blemish the reputation of that public servant who help me steal the window. It's now in my daughter's home on Galveston Island.

———

Some Christmases, Mimi would go visit her other daughter, Lou Green, in Louisiana, and when she wasn't with us, we never fixed the traditional Christmas turkey dinner. Instead we'd have fried oysters and guacamole salad. Some of our friends thought that menu was a trifle weird for Christmas but both our kids thought it was wonderful and Mary Helen and I agreed.

What got us started on the oysters is that once in a while when I was chasing stories along the Texas coast I'd stop in Matagorda, at the mouth of the Colorado River, and bring home a gallon of fresh-shucked oysters. I always felt the Colorado was one of the cleanest streams in our part of the world and that the bay water it flowed into produced the finest oysters. I remember paying $10 a gallon for the first Matagorda oysters I bought. That had to be in about 1950. If I bought a gallon of those babies now I would need to pay them out by the month.

If you say it fast a gallon of oysters doesn't sound like very many but it always fed the four of us that festive Christmas meal with a couple of dozen left over for the next day. We'd start out eating them raw, about a dozen each, with saltine crackers and a piquant red sauce. Then we'd switch to fried, with the guacamole salad.

Since only the immediate family was involved, we didn't have to be formal but eventually we did become ceremonial about this feast. Our own private ceremony. Only three of us were seated at a time. Mary Helen and I took turns frying oysters and dishing them out sizzling hot. One of Mary Helen's theories about cooking, and one I certainly endorsed, was that if food is supposed to be hot, be certain it's not served cold.

We had fun with this oyster Christmas and before we left the table we always talked about our friend Marie Moore, because the guacamole was made with her recipe. I sat elbow to elbow with Marie's husband John for five years at the *Houston Post* and the Moores and the Hales had their first offspring at about the same time. Every year we'd repeat Marie's story about how she bought avocados when they were first showing up in Texas grocery stores. She'd find a few soft ones that were just right for guacamole and go to the man in the produce department and say, "These things are almost rotten," and he'd sell them to her for half price.

We dipped the guacamole with king-sized corn chips. We ate the hot fried oysters with squeezes of fresh-cut lemon. A fine Christmas dinner.

While I was working on this book, just before Christmas of '98, I called my son in Wichita, Kansas and asked what he was doing. He was fixing a batch of hot cheese dip, the kind his mother taught him to make when he was twelve years old. On Christmas Eve I called my daughter and asked what she was having for dinner the next day. She said, "Fried oysters and guacamole salad."

# New York Café Beef Enchiladas

This recipe is from Phyllis and Jimmy Miniatis. Maybe one reason it didn't taste exactly like I remembered was because they used bacon grease when they cooked 'em for me, instead of lard. The comments on the chili part are from Phyllis; the directions on assembly are in Jimmy's words, told to Phyllis.

## New York Café Chili

3 lbs. coarsely ground meat
½ lb. lard
2 T. chili powder
4 T. paprika
2 crushed garlic cloves
2 T. ground cumin seed (comino)

*Render the lard in a pan, add the meat and brown it.*
*Add the spices.*
*Cover with water and cook slowly, stirring occasionally.*
*In another pan, cook two cups of red (pinto) beans with*
*½ T. comino and 1 T. paprika. Cook one hour.*
*Put in blender or mixer and process ("like mashed potatoes").*
*Add mashed beans to chili. ("Remember! No tomato sauce.")*

*Assembling the enchiladas:*

*Chili (as above)*
*Large skillet*
*Vegetable oil*
*Corn tortillas*
*Chopped onion*
*Rat trap cheese*
*Metal plates (that can withstand broiler heat)*

*Take a large skillet. Pour in thin layer of vegetable oil (about ¼ inch). Heat the oil until hot—not sizzling. Take corn tortillas and drop in the hot oil. Leave for a few seconds until tortillas are soft and pliable. Blot with paper towel.*
*Lay one tortilla on a flat surface. Spread a thin line of onions in center of tortilla. On top of onions place a tablespoon of hot chili and a thin layer of rat trap cheese.*
*Roll the tortilla around its contents into a tight roll. Place three of these tortillas side by side in a metal plate. (Three to an order.)*
*On top of these three enchiladas, spread more onions. Then cover with a liberal layer of chili and then top with rat trap cheese.*
*Place the metal plate of enchiladas under the broiler until all the cheese has melted and is bubbling.*
*Serve.*

## Fried Matagorda Oysters

The commentary here is from daughter Becky Hale Fisher.

*A quantity of fresh, shucked Matagorda (or other top
   quality) oysters
Salt
Cayenne pepper
Ground white pepper
Corn meal
Cooking oil
Deep pot with fry basket or deep frying pan and slotted
   spoon
Lemon wedges*

*Rinse the oysters in a colander and drain.*
*Add seasonings to corn meal and dredge the oysters in the
meal. Don't let oysters sit after dredging. Coat as you fry.*
*Drop oysters in hot oil. Make sure the oil is hot enough. The
only way to mess up fried oysters is to drop them in oil that
isn't hot enough. They should bubble vigorously immediately
when submerged in the oil.*
*Fry for about three minutes. They float when they're ready.
A golden brown color is what you want to see.*
*The oysters should be crispy on the outside and juicy on the
inside.*

## Marie Moore's Guacamole Salad

*4 large very ripe avocados, or 6 small ones*
*1 clove fresh garlic*
*1 T. salt*
*1 large lime*
*2 average-sized ripe tomatoes*
*4 small green onions*

*In the bottom of a mixing bowl, mash the clove of garlic together with the tablespoon of salt. Peel avocados and save one big seed. Cut avocado meat into bite sizes.*
*Squeeze the juice of the lime over the pieces, and mash with a fork. Do not use a blender on guacamole. Leave it slightly lumpy, to preserve avocado flavor.*
*Mash the ripe tomatoes, chopped green onions and crushed garlic into the avocado. Add salt with caution and keep tasting. Remember the guacamole probably will be eaten with salted corn chips so watch out for too much salt.*

# *Mark Hale's Hot* Queso

*2 large, ripe, fresh jalapenos,*
*1 can Rotel tomatoes (whole, not pieces) with juice*
*4 oz. of Velveeta processed cheese*
*6 oz. of American processed cheese (slices are fine);*
*Tortilla chips or fritos*

*Chop the jalapenos. Chop the Rotel tomatoes.*
*Cut the cheese into chunks so it can melt easily.*
*Add the tomatoes and jalapenos to the cheese and melt the*
*cheese.*
*(You can either melt the cheese in a saucepan on the stove,*
*taking care not to burn; or place all the ingredients in a bowl*
*and melt in the microwave.)*
*This should not be too runny. To thicken, add more*
*American cheese; or take the heated mixture and place in the*
*freezer for five minutes before serving.*
*Serve with tortilla chips or Fritos.*

# Mimi's Orange Ambrosia

This recipe comes from Koleen Vick, Mimi's daughter-in-law.

*2 coconuts*
*3 large cans of sliced pineapples; reserve the juice;*
*3 dozen good navel oranges; reserve the juice;*
*Granulated sugar*

*Dice the sliced pineapple. Peel and dice the oranges. Peel and halve the coconuts. Reserve the coconut milk. Cut the coconut into chunks and grate. (Mind your knuckles.)*

*In a glass baking dish, layer one-third of the pineapple, one-third of the oranges; and one-third of the coconut; distribute one-third cup of sugar over all. Repeat layers until all ingredients have been used.*

*Combine the reserved orange and pineapple juice with the reserved coconut milk and pour the liquid over contents of the bowl.*

*Refrigerate overnight, or until well chilled.*

*Serve in crystal compotes.*

## Mimi's Pancakes

1 cup flour
1 tsp. baking powder
½ tsp. baking soda
1 tsp. sugar
½ tsp. salt
1 egg
1 cup buttermilk, room temperature
1 T. cooking oil

Add the baking soda to the butter milk. Lightly beat the egg together with the oil and add to the buttermilk/soda mixture.
Mix the remaining dry ingredients together.
Pour liquid ingredients, as mixed, into the dry ingredients and combine lightly.
This should be a thin batter to make tender, thin pancakes.
Cook on a hot griddle, taking care to keep pancakes no more than three inches in diameter.

## Mimi's Chicken and Dumplings

This recipe has passed down to my daughter, Becky.

*Boil chicken. It can be either whole, breasts, or whatever you like. Boil with celery, onion, garlic, salt, pepper and any other seasonings you fancy. The stock needs to have flavor. (Editor's note: Look for organic, free range chickens which are now available in many stores.)*
*Reserve the stock.*

*For the dumplings:*
*2 cups flour*
*1 tsp. salt*
*⅔ cup shortening ("I know it's a lot," says Becky.)*
*1 tsp. baking powder*

*Sift together dry ingredients. Cut shortening into the dry mixture until it looks like cornmeal. Add water (start with ¼ cup) and stir with a fork until it gathers into a ball. Roll out dough and cut into long strips.*
*Bring reserved chicken stock to a rolling boil. Add the chicken. Drop in dumpling strips and cook uncovered for five minutes. Stock should be boiling, but "don't boil them to death."*
*Lower heat to simmer or low, cover and cook until tender, about twenty minutes.*
*Some people don't add the chicken to the stock along with the dumplings. They prefer to serve it on the side.*

# Camp
# Cookery

*T*here's a mysterious Voice deep inside men that frequently whispers, "Leave home. Go forth into the wilderness, cook, and eat." I don't entirely understand this compulsion, despite that I've obeyed the Voice hundreds of times.

When we were in third grade my friend Robert Childress and I used to take meat and bread up on a rocky hillside near our homes and build a fire and heat whatever we had. We'd sit up there and chew and look out at the clouds and mesquite trees and if anybody had asked why, we wouldn't have been able to say.

Later on Dude Wilkins and I shot and cooked and ate those jaybirds that time, and we were around fifteen then.

For twenty years my old friend Gene Morgan of Sweeny would go with me every March to South Texas to meet spring, and we always took a couple of dozen tamales. Somewhere down the road we'd pull off and build a fire and heat those babies and eat them with crackers and ketchup. We had money in our pockets and we'd pass restaurants every ten miles but still we felt the need to fix something to eat out-doors, on the road. I think we were responding to the Voice.

In 1970 when we were all close to fifty, three friends and I took a trip of hundreds of miles into the South Texas Brush Country and that entire expedition had to do with little more than eating. We planned for weeks, arguing about dates and meeting places and running up phone bills and in all those preliminaries, food or cooking wasn't even mentioned. And yet, I can't think now of any other reason we went.

Culp Krueger, former Texas state senator, was the leader of that adventure, mainly because when he took part in an enterprise he wasn't interested in being anything other then the leader. Krueger was a stocky, tight-wound person with intense feelings about almost everything. He wore his hair long, senatorial style. In the Texas Senate he is remembered for making impassioned speeches, bowing low at the end and straightening up sharply, so his hair would fly overhead in a spectacular way.

He came to our meeting place from El Campo. Merck Smith from Olivia. Ralph Stockton from Louise. I joined them from Houston and we loaded into a small van and rolled down the highway, looking for things to eat.

Say we came to a city of moderate size. Krueger sat in the right front seat, scouting for cafés. He loved adventurous eating.

Here's a couple of fast food places.

He'd say, *No, no, go on.*

Here's a highway steak house.

*No, never.*

Here on the courthouse square is a large family restaurant, looking locally owned.

*No. Turn left*, Krueger would say, and soon we'd be bouncing down in the ragged end of town where the streets weren't paved and boys would be playing baseball in the dust.

Close to the railroad tracks we'd see a squatty flat-topped building with a screen door entry and Johnson grass and tall weeds growing along its side. Two old cars parked in front. And a sign. Lupe's Café.

*Stop here,* Krueger would say. *That's what we want.*

He'd lead the way in. Three wood tables, set with knives and forks wrapped in paper napkins. Four high stools at a short counter. Drivers of the cars out front on the stools, drinking beer. Krueger would go right on back to the kitchen and meet Lupé herself and brag on how clean everything was and how good the kitchen smelled. He'd ask about her children and her husband and about business and he'd ask if she could fix us, for starters, a great big platter of chili con queso.

*Si, si, si.* Sit down, *señores, por favor.*

We might stay in Lupe's two and a half hours, eating tamales and tacos and enchiladas and refried beans and guacamole salad.

Sometimes it would be wonderful food. But at a few of those adventurous places Krueger enjoyed, the adventure challenged my appetite. I remember a little place down close to the Mexican border, near Laredo, where we ate huevos rancheros while the proprietor stood guard over our table. He was armed with a fly swatter. If a fly landed beside your plate—whap—proprietor would dispatch that insect and flick its remains off on the floor.

Krueger was a fine camp cook. His specialty was a huge pot roast, with beef and almost every vegetable known to truck farmers. On that food trip into South Texas we stayed a couple of nights at a cabin that Stockton maintained on a deer lease, about eight miles out in the brush from Pearsall. In a

Pearsall grocery store we stocked up on what I thought was enough grub to last a week, and we drove out there in the bushes and cooked it and ate it.

All three of those guys are gone now. I wish I had the recipe for the pot roast that Krueger fixed. He'd dish it up in deep bowls and put one down in front of you and say, "There. Now what's wrong with that?" And nothing at all was wrong with it.

Several years passed before that scene in the hunting cabin began to strike me as curious. Four middle-aged guys, way out there in the brush, doing nothing but cooking and eating. Hunting? Nobody in the foursome carried as much as a cap pistol. We stayed out there until we ate everything we brought, and then came back home. A classic case of the Voice, speaking to men. "Go forth in the wilderness, and cook, and eat."

In the spring of 1982 I received an invitation from Bill Shearer, who was my book publisher, to go on a fishing and camping trip out in the Texas Hill Country, in the Llano River Valley.

Five of us went, that first time. We slept in bedrolls on a half-acre of flat rock and cooked on a campfire and stayed three nights.

Nobody planned a menu for any of those days. In the little city of Mason, we stopped at a grocery store because we'd heard it had wooden floors and bananas hanging from a stalk, the way they were displayed in stores when we were all young. We bought enough stuff that we thought would last us for the trip, and went on to the river.

The first night we had beef stew that Bill's wife Kathy made and froze for us, to thaw out on the camp fire. The second night we grilled hamburgers, and ate on the great pot of pinto beans we kept going for three days. The third and last night we fried the fish we had caught. We had baloney and rat trap cheese in the beer coolers, in case we didn't catch enough fish for Saturday supper. Scrambled eggs for breakfast every morning.

The next spring we returned to that same flat rock, stayed three nights again, and ate exactly the same menu. Stew on Thursday, burgers on Wednesday, fish on Saturday. Scrambled eggs for all breakfasts, and pinto beans twenty-four hours a day. Lunch was every man for himself. Baloney sandwiches or more beans or do without.

If we gather on the river again the spring of 2000, we'll have returned to that same place eighteen consecutive years, to fish the same water and eat the same chow.

The personnel has changed. Two of the original guys have died, and both were key members. Bill Shearer died of a brain tumor at forty-six. And cancer got Fred Whitehead of Austin when he was not much older. Loss of those two almost cancelled our trip permanently, since Shearer was the organizer of the trip and Whitehead was the most dedicated fisherman and the chief camp cook.

But we carried on, in a weakened condition, and gradually across the years we've built back strength. Shearer's son Travis began going to the river with us when he was a skinny kid in the second grade. Suddenly he is six feet tall and 175 pounds and he and his friend Josh Kramer set trotlines and catch catfish, so we won't have to eat baloney sandwiches Saturday night. And we've added Fred Whitehead's brother Glenn who may be a better cook than Fred. The others of us serve mainly as the pep squad and gofers when it comes to preparing food on the river.

Camp cooks are like softball pitchers. They need constant encouragement and praise. I mean if you're handed a plate of food on a river bank you need to say it's nothing south of wonderful. You must never, ever, criticize camp grub because the cook can lay down his ladle, tell everybody to go straight on to hell, and walk away. I have seen it happen.

This need that camp cooks have for praise was a factor in the only significant change we've had in our menu in eighteen years on the river.

In the beginning I was a sort of sous-chef, behind Whitehead, and later his brother Glenn. I was allowed to cook the pinto beans, under supervision, and I fixed hamburgers on Friday night. I invested a lot of effort in the preparation of those burgers. Since I couldn't find the kind of hamburger I wanted at the grocery store where we bought most of our food, I always took meat from home.

On Tuesday in Houston I bought meat that wouldn't be cooked until the next Friday at sundown, and it had to travel 300 miles in my pickup so I figured it needed to be frozen. On Tuesday night I fixed quarter-pound patties and arranged them between plastic wrapping and left them in the freezer overnight.

We were feeding a dozen guys at this time and they'd be stray-dog hungry, coming off the river from fishing all day, so I fixed two patties for each man. That's twenty-four patties, and then I fixed an extra dozen. Because one or two of those dudes would walk up and grab a patty off the grill and wolf it down without even fixing a burger. "That's my appetizer," he'd say, and have the guts to tell me it needed more salt.

Making thirty-six patties is not a terrible job but it's not something you can do with one hand while you read the funnies.

One day back in the mid-1980s I was feeling a little wild and I ordered a dozen steaks from an outfit up in Kansas City. They came frozen in a big thick tight-lidded Styrofoam container. That container was more useful to me than the steaks. I found a rectangular cook pan that fit the bottom of the Styro chest. I'd fill the pan with water and let it stay in the freezer two or three days, until the water froze hard as sidewalks. Then nurse that slab of ice out of the pan and drop it in the bottom of the chest and stack the frozen patties on top and duct-tape that sucker airtight. By Friday when I needed them that meat would still be partly frozen.

I'm telling you this just to show how much trouble I went to, providing hamburgers for that gang on the river.

For ten years I did hamburgers that way. I sliced the tomatoes and onions and pickles and put out the buns and the mustard and mayo and potato chips and then stood in the smoke from the grill and cooked. And in all the years I did that, I didn't hear one word of praise for my hamburgers.

So I quit.

The eleventh year we were on the river, Friday about sundown somebody in the bunch said, "Hey, this is hamburger day. Where's those hamburgers?"

I said I didn't know, and they said, "You mean you're not gonna do hamburgers this time?"

"That's right, I'm not."

"How come?"

Aha. "Because," I said, "I've been doing those hamburgers out here for ten damn years, and not a one of you sons of bitches ever said a nice thing about them."

They all laughed then, and nodded, because they understood well enough the rule about praising the camp cook. For two years after that they tried to get me to do Friday hamburgers again. They'd say those burgers I used to cook were sure good, and they wished I'd do them again. But I have refused. That was praise too late. They had their chance and missed it.

Why no, they didn't get mad at me for calling them sons of bitches. We are all friends, and can call one another the worst of names and it's understood that the insults mustn't be taken literally. This has been customary among all the close-friend groups of men I've ever known, and many women don't understand it. Such name-calling is a curious kind of masculine endearment. It's saying, "I can insult you and you won't be wounded because we are friends and we love one another."

However, a few insensitive men violate this code, before a sound friendship has been established. I once heard a fellow speak of a man he had known only a few weeks, and said he didn't like the guy. Why? The answer was, "He called me a son of a bitch too soon."

My Friday hamburgers have been replaced by Glenn Whitehead's fajitas which he serves with an excellent sauce he makes fresh on the river bank. He brings all the ingredients from his home in Smithville, where his art studio is, and spends hours chopping and slicing and dicing and cussing.

## *Roll Your Own Fajitas*

Glenn points out that this is the perfect meal to eat around a campfire—no knives, forks or plates needed.

He prefers flank steak to the usual skirt steak for this feast because it's "thicker, cooks more evenly and will probably be more tender." For six hungry campers, he recommends two to two-and-one-half pounds of flank steak which he marinates in four tablespoons of olive oil, and four tablespoons of soy sauce.

"Sometimes," he says, "I spike the marinade with Vietnamese chili garlic sauce, a bright red concoction which is hot as hell. Sometimes I toss in sliced onions. I've also used Worcestershire sauce, Italian dressing, Tabasco sauce or even Chinese black bean sauce. It's not important what you use."

He dusts the meat liberally with garlic powder and meat tenderizer before putting it into the marinade. "Use a dish that allows the meat to lie flat and soak up the marinade. I use a two-inch-deep baking dish. Let the meat lie in the marinade in the refrigerator for two or three hours, turning it once. You can do this before you leave home, then put the meat with a little of the marinade into a plastic zip-lock freezer bag and store it in your ice chest."

He cooks the meat on a little travel grill he brings with him, but any kind of fire will do. This is Glenn talking: "With a flank steak, I like to start off cooking hot, that way searing and sealing the meat, and then I move the meat to a place on the grill where flame-ups are less likely. Even so, it's hard to imagine cooking much longer that fifteen or twenty minutes.

"One bit of advice to the cooker: don't leave your post. Stay. If you're in charge of the meat and worried about the grave responsibility put on your shoulders, remember you are there to protect it from burning. Turn it with a fork or tongs. Frequent turns don't hurt and may keep the meat juicier. When it's done the meat ought to be crispy on the outside and real pink and juicy in the middle. It's as simple as that."

Glenn's ingredients for his salsa—which some people will say resembles *pico de gallo*—include fifteen large jalapenos, seeded and diced; the juice of four to six limes; six to eight Roma tomatoes, diced; one bunch of fresh cilantro, chopped. No onion. He feels that onion overpowers the salsa.

He handles the peppers bare-handed, taking care to touch them with only one hand. By the time you're done, he says, "the hand that has been handling the sliced jalapenos might be on fire. Baking soda may help douse it. Me, I sort of like to feel that burn. I regard it as something of a badge of courage, or at least, duty."

When the peppers have been diced, he squeezes the juice from two of the limes over them. "The lime juice tames the heat of the jalapenos somewhat, so sequence is important. Let the peppers sit in a bowl with the lime juice while you dice the tomatoes, then add them to the bowl.

"Next rinse the cilantro, shake off the excess water and chop the leaves. Be extravagant about throwing away stems. Add the chopped cilantro to the other ingredients in the bowl, mix, taste and adjust proportions as necessary. I usually add more of everything. It is not possible to have too much salsa. That is a fact."

The remaining ingredients for his fajitas include eighteen to twenty-four flour tortillas, three cans of black beans, a bag of shredded cheese, any kind—cheddar, Monterey Jack, Swiss, even a mixture of parmesan and provolone.

About the beans: "It's not as simple as you think. You don't just open the cans and heat the beans. Nope, because some damned fool has packed the beans in a thick slippery, starchy goo which can turn a perfectly good fajita into a soggy mess. I empty the canned beans into a colander and rinse with cold water, gently stirring them." He sprinkles a little ground cumin and pepper and salt over the beans, but you don't have to heat them, unless you want to.

Glenn likes to warm the tortillas in a frying pan. "Over low flame, just a tiny bit of butter to prevent sticking. I stack six to ten tortillas in the pan and keep flipping them and cutting the deck, as it were, breaking the stack at the middle, turning the top three or four, then flipping the whole stack. That way the tortillas are heating, not burning. It only takes three or four minutes.

"When ready to serve, slice the meat across the grain. Thin slivers are best. Thick slices are apt to pull out of the fajita, collapsing its structural integrity. With fajitas, structural integrity is important."

Service is simple, even for a campsite. "Serve the meat on the cutting board where you sliced it," he says. "Place a stack of flour tortillas and a bowl of salsa next to the meat (plus, if you wish, the optional bowl of beans), open a bag of shredded cheese, and then it's every man for himself." Just don't overstuff a tortilla. "There's no rescuing a fajita spilled outdoors."

——

Our accommodations for this trip have improved, since the beginning. The first three years we all met at a rally point and drove into the Hill Country in a Volkswagen van, so overloaded it had trouble climbing the modest highway slopes out west of Austin. We slept in bedrolls on that great flat rock and talked about how wonderful it was to lie there at night under the stars. Come morning most of us would have trouble straightening up, from sleeping on that stone.

About the fourth year one of our bunch came to the river in his pickup with a mattress in its bed, and the fifth year, without any advance planning, every man came in his own vehicle with something to sleep on that was softer than a rock.

Cooking could be a problem at that campsite, too. I remember a Saturday when we were trying to fry fish and the wind was blowing so hard it whipped the very grease out of the skillet, and when you took a bite of fish you got a lot of gritty stuff in your mouth. Whitehead would say, "That's the cornmeal I rolled the fish in." But it seemed a lot more like dirt.

Texas weather in April and May can get mighty hot and we had no shade on that big flat rock. Once we brought along a big plastic tarp and rigged a sort of tent, so we could get out of the sun to eat. Worked all morning putting the thing up. Just when we were ready to sit under it, a blustering wind came around a bend and blew the whole concern down the river.

So we found a new campsite that had lots of shade trees, and used that spot two or three years. The only trouble was, the stream bank there had such a slope to it you couldn't put a can of beer on the ground without its tipping over and spilling, and for our bunch that was a serious matter. Wasting beer couldn't be tolerated because the closest place to buy more was fifteen miles away and half of that distance was dirt road.

Then once we got rained on pretty bad and had to pack up and leave early, and another year the river rose and threatened to wash us away and we were obliged to pick up and run.

So we were truly pleased when we were offered the use of a

large camp house, just downstream from the great flat rock. That place might not look pretty to a reader of Architectural Digest but to us, it's beautiful. Because it has a kitchen with a four-burner electric stove. It has a big refrigerator and a freezer and hot and cold running water and a flock of bunk beds and a roof that doesn't leak much. But the greatest improvement is a flushable toilet. By this time, most of the fishermen in our bunch were agreeing that going to the bathroom in the bushes had lost its entertainment value.

So that camp house is where we've fished and fixed our meals for the last several years, and the owners won't even let us pay rent.

A funny thing, though. Every year when we go to the camp we like to walk up the river to that big flat rock and stay a while and talk about those first few years when we underwent all the hardships, for reasons we'd have trouble explaining.

*Here's where we tried to anchor one of the posts of the tent that the wind blew away. Here's what's left of the ring of rocks where we cooked, and where the wind blew the grease out of the skillet that time. And the beans turned blue in the pot and we didn't know why, and that big old white dog—what kind of dog? Great Pyrennes? That son of a gun walked up out of the brush after dark and started eating out of the stew pot and we never did know where he came from, remember that?*

*Hey, remember that heavy grill we cooked on? Hell of a grill. Spraddled the whole fire. It was a drag they used to smooth the softball field out back of Shearer's place in Fredericksburg. Wonder whatever happened to that grill.*

*Right here on this rock is where two or three of us got our first lesson on handling a fly rod. From some pretty good teachers, too, like Fred Whitehead and John Graves. And here's where Rusty Mitchum showed us how he could fix a hot cobbler in a* cast iron pot on the campfire, using canned fruit and biscuit dough and soda water and I don't remember what else. And down below the crossing was where old Glenn Bass hooked a cottonmouth moccasin on a bass plug, and came walking into camp with that snake, like he'd caught something we could cook for supper. Remember that?

## Rusty Mitchum's Riverbank Peach Cobbler

There are two varieties Rusty makes, one with tortillas, one with soda pop. The tortilla version comes first, in Rusty's own words.

*To start off, you need a 12-inch cast iron Dutch oven. That seems to be just the right size for parties of five to twenty-five. The best kind is the one with legs and a lid that has a lip around it to hold your coals in place.*

*When you purchase your oven, first you scrub it real good with hot soapy water. Next coat the oven inside and out with some kind of vegetable shortening and place it and its lid upside down in your kitchen oven and set the temp at 350 degrees. Leave it in there for an hour or so, then shut off the heat and let it cool. The Dutch oven is considered "seasoned" at this point, but I like to run it through the procedure a couple of more times, just to make sure. Then I fry some bacon in the oven a few times to really get it seasoned. From this point on whenever you clean your oven, use scalding hot water and scrub it out. Never use soap or a metal scouring pad, because this will remove your seasoning. Now you are ready to make some cobbler.*

*4-6 No. 2 cans of sliced peaches*
*½ cup of sugar*
*Ground cinnamon*
*A 1-inch thick stack of flour tortillas*
*1 stick of butter or margarine*
*Charcoal*

*Heat 20-36 charcoal briquettes until hot; use 6-8 of the briquettes to make a small bed of coals; reserve fourteen to eighteen of the hot coals for use on the lid of the Dutch oven;*
*Drain the peaches and pour them into the Dutch oven. Sprinkle some cinnamon on them and stir it in.*
*Take the stack of tortillas and cut them into one inch strips; mix three-quarters of them in with the peaches.*
*Cover the mixture with the remaining strips of tortillas.*
*Mix a couple of teaspoons of cinnamon with the sugar and spread on top of the tortillas; dot with thin pats of butter.*
*Place the Dutch oven on the small bed of coals.*
*Place the lid on the oven and cover it with fourteen to eighteen hot coals.*
*Cook for around thirty to forty-five minutes, until the top layer of tortillas starts to brown.*
*Spoon out some into a bowl and get after it. Be careful, though. Straight out of the Dutch oven it will be so hot it'll take the hair off your tongue.*

*This amount will feed fifteen to twenty people.*

# Rusty's Peach Cobbler with Cake Mix and Soda Pop

Again, in Rusty's words.

*4-6 No. 2 cans of sliced peaches*
*Ground cinnamon*
*One box of white or yellow cake mix*
*One can of Sprite*

*Drain the peaches and pour them into the Dutch oven. Sprinkle some cinnamon on the peaches and stir it in. Next sprinkle the cake mix on top of the peaches. Then pour the Sprite over the cake mix. Use the top of the peach can to mix the Sprite with the cake mix.*

*Place the lid on the Dutch oven and place it on a small bed of coals, with hot charcoal briquettes on the lid, just like the previous version. It will take between thirty to forty-five minutes to cook, but you need to check it every so often. The cake will rise and start to turn brown. Then it's ready to eat.*

*This amount will feed fifteen to twenty people.*

## Rosario Borrego's Pork Tamales

Rosario and Vicente Borrego and their children are Old Friend Morgan's family.

*For 8 dozen tamales:*
*Cut an 8 pound pork roast into pieces and stew with onions and salt until it is thoroughly cooked; Drain and shred into bowl. Save the broth in which the meat was cooked.*
*Mix cayenne, cumin powder, salt and fresh garlic in a blender. Mix these spices into the drained meat and set aside.*
*Simmer 8 dozen corn shucks in water.*
*For each dozen tamales, cut a little lard into one pound of* masa harina *and moisten with the reserved meat broth until it forms a ball; let it rest for a little while.*
*Remove the corn shucks from the water and clean off any remaining silks or fibers. Lay the shucks flat.*
*Put a little spoonful of the* masa *mixture into each shuck and flatten it.*
*Put a little spoonful of the meat mixture into the center of the flattened masa and fold edges of the shuck over each other like a taco, tucking the bottom end inside the fold.*
*When all the tamales are assembled, add a little water to a large pot and heat.*
*Place the tamales, standing on their folded ends, into a steamer and set over the simmering water. Steam for 30-35 minutes.*
*Eat immediately, or freeze and enjoy later, reheated.*
*Can be topped with chili con carne or eaten on their own.*

# The Catfish Chowder Event

*T*he letter was beautifully written. In my work I've read a ton of mail and I have developed a great admiration for a well-written letter. That may be because I've read so many bad ones, and because the good ones are so rare.

The message in her letter was that she was writing a piece of fiction and one of her characters was a Texan and she was having trouble with the way the fellow talked, in her dialogue. He didn't sound genuine. She wondered if I'd do her the favor of having lunch, so she could hear me talk. Because she thought the voice she heard in my column sounded like a genuine Texan and she had not been around many genuine Texans recently.

Writers do that sort of thing. It comes under the heading of research. And I counted it at least a mild compliment that a writer would want to hear me talk.

At this time I was in that footloose period of my life, living in the bachelor apartment. I was still making Soupwiches then, so I seldom went out for lunch. Also at that time of day I was often fighting a deadline.

187

But I happened to notice the letter showed a River Oaks return address. I was not accustomed to getting lunch invitations from ladies in River Oaks, where the houses tend to have fourteen rooms and six and a half baths and curving driveways. But it helped me understand the letter. A writer could, indeed, live in River Oaks for years without hearing very much of a Texas drawl. I had done some work in that part of Houston and it seemed to me the majority of folks there talked as if they came from Connecticut, or at least Massachusetts. Also I decided that what the writer really meant to say in the letter was that she wanted to hear a *rural* Texan talk. And that's what I am. I began that way and haven't changed much because I can't.

I am telling you all this because it has a great deal to do with food, including practically everything I've eaten since the day I went to lunch with the writer of that letter.

Figuring a River Oaks woman would want to eat in a fancy restaurant, I dressed pretty well up. However, we went to an ordinary place and I ordered a hot beef sandwich. In the highway cafes I often patronized, this dish was made up of leftover meat and potatoes distributed over a couple of slices of stale bread and slathered in thick brown gravy. She looked at it and her mouth twitched at one corner, as if it wanted to grin. She ordered some kind of lady food, with greenery and fruit.

I'll go ahead and tell you that this woman was a perfect dish. Long black hair with narrow streaks of premature gray at the sides. An oval Elizabeth Taylor-type face. Dark eyes and creamy smooth skin and features that I thought were, well, sort of aristocratic, intelligent. I've always thought intelligence is attractive, even on a homely face, and on a beautiful face it's almost intimidating.

My guess on her age was twenty-eight. She said she was thirty-seven and divorced and had a son seven-years-old. We visited a long time so she could hear me talk, although it did seem to me I did a lot more listening than talking. Out in the parking lot before we separated she asked if I liked music. I said I did, practically all kinds, except for this crazy stuff where the kids in the band dress up funny and their instruments are wired for sound that'll break out windows and you can feel their beat from a block away. She nodded and said, Well, maybe some time if I went out to listen to some music and wanted company, she could go along. I said fine and left. I supposed she was just being polite.

For about a month I didn't hear anything out of her. Then I had a message on my answer machine that said she'd been off on a trip and was back in town. That's all it said, that she was back. I didn't know she'd been gone.

I thought, Maybe she wants to hear some more rural Texas speech. So I wrote her a note and said I was going to see my old friend Blackie Clark. He lived at Richmond on the bank of the Brazos River and he was one of the best rural Texas talkers I knew, and maybe the foremost storyteller in all this state. Would she like to go with me and listen to Blackie?

I could have called her instead of writing. I think now I wrote instead of calling because I didn't want to hear her say no, or force her to invent some thin excuse.

She called and said she'd be pleased to go see Blackie.

It was one of those perfect calm soft-sunny November days we sometimes get in Texas. I was a hero to Blackie, bringing that beautiful woman to the river to hear him talk. He was inspired, and talked and talked. Before we left he said to her, "Honey, you're the prettiest thing that ever walked through my front gate." She didn't seem bothered by being referred to as a thing.

We needed to eat. I stopped at a drive-in joint on the highway and she ordered a hamburger all the way, pickles, onions, mustard, fries, everything, and finished it before I could eat mine. She said it was one of the best burgers she ever ate. But I wasn't entirely convinced. Maybe she's just saying that, to make me comfortable.

We got back into Houston about dark and I needed to go to the apartment and feed and walk a dog I was keeping for a friend. She said she'd like to go along, see where I lived.

That apartment was terrible. It was a mess. Look out the windows of that place and you saw a solid stone wall less than twenty feet away.

She liked the apartment. She even liked the friend's dog, which I had always thought was an ill-humored little bastard. She looked out the window and saw interesting patterns of shadow on the stone wall, cast by lights from across the street. I showed her pictures of my children, both within a few years of her own age. She said they were beautiful. She looked in my miniature kitchen and asked me if I cooked. From the first she seemed really interested in food. I told her about my pinto beans and my Soupwich and she said the beans sounded all right. When I took her home she gave me a hug. A pretty tight one, too, and it made me thoughtful.

Over the next few days I did a lot of talking to myself. Look, pal, you're riding toward trouble. You don't have any business getting mixed up with this woman. To begin with, even if she's old as she says, you're still talking about twenty-plus years difference in age, an entire generation. Furthermore, she grew up in that River Oaks culture and you don't fit there.

Since I'd moved into the apartment I'd met a couple of

ladies, nice round ones, closer to my own age. We'd gone to movies, and sedate dances, and restaurants where they served meatloaf and fried chicken and pecan pie. I told myself if you intend to walk into a serious involvement, you ought to forget this young one and take up with one of those women closer to your own speed.

She went on another trip somewhere, and while she was gone I did some detective work. The facts I uncovered were even worse than I had imagined.

To begin with, she had never in her life been in a public school. She had attended expensive private schools and taken a degree from Sweet Briar, that fancy girls' college in Virginia. And damned if she wasn't one of those debutantes, girls that come out, as they call it, and get their pictures in the paper just for growing up and looking pretty and having mamas and papas with nice bank accounts.

From other sources I learned she had done graduate work at Rice University, one of the toughest schools in creation to get into. She had lived two years in England and studied at London School of Economics and traveled extensively over Europe. She spoke French.

And I found out why she had grinned at my hot beef sandwich. She had been a magazine restaurant critic and was then doing restaurant consulting for the famous Brennan family of New Orleans.

The voice that speaks to me sometimes, when I'm faced with decisions, was saying I'd be making a five-star mistake to pursue this woman. Not just because of the age difference. I came out of a Great Depression cornbread-and-beans culture and I'd never really left it, and she was River Oaks and Sweet Briar and London and Paris. The voice told me there was no way I'd ever bridge a gap that wide.

However, that hug she'd given me had a lingering effect. It wouldn't go away. I decided I at least ought to find out what it meant. Sometimes a guy can get hugged and it feels a lot better than the hugger intends for it to feel. Hugs like that need analysis and interpretation because they're capable of causing trouble.

While I was pondering this matter I got a call from my friend Buck Sloan, country singer and guitar picker and organizer of interesting events. A month before, he had organized a float trip down the Trinity River, all the way from Dallas to Trinity Bay, and he'd asked if I wanted to go along and write about the adventure. Two or three boatloads of guys, camping on sand bars, eating nothing but what they could catch out of the river. The kind of thing I love. It turned out I wasn't able to go but I told Buck when they got near the end of the float, find a town and a telephone and call me and I'd meet them on the river and listen to the tales of the trip.

A couple of weeks later he called from about a hundred miles upstream and said they'd camp the next Tuesday night near the Highway 90 Trinity Bridge at Liberty, about forty miles east of Houston. He said come eat supper with the bunch there on the river, that they'd fix just whatever they'd caught that day. He said bring a friend if I wanted to.

So I asked her to go, not really certain whether I wanted her to say yes or no. Why would a consultant in the field of fancy restaurants want to eat on a river bank with a gang of guys who'd been sleeping on sand bars for three weeks?

She said she'd love to go.

I was a hero for bringing that pretty woman to the river. All those old boys, who must have been bone tired from that trip, lifted their shoulders and straightened their backs and walked around all full of strength and energy and told their stories with grinning faces and shining eyes and we all had a fine meeting there on the river. Then came time to eat and here's what happened:

She sat on a stump and ate catfish chowder out of a syrup bucket and said it was wonderful.

That did it for me. I stopped worrying about the twenty-three years age difference and the culture gap and all the other obstacles. And since that little picnic on the river, that woman and I have never been separated more than a few days.

We began cooking together, trying at first to reproduce the flavor of the chowder we ate on the Trinity with Buck. We made stews, and omelettes. She had these wonderful individual omelette pans that belonged to her mother and I loved watching her fold the eggs in the pans and take them off the fire just at the right time so they wouldn't be too done or too raw.

I showed her how I do my pinto beans, and she cooked cornbread to go with them and made them better. We cooked chicken and dumplings, and pancakes the way I've always liked them, small and thin and kept hot in a warming oven so they could be eaten two at a time and nobody ever got a cold one.

She knew how to rescue food that was cooking and threatening failure. For example, once when she was at one of those meetings and book reviews she was always attending I decided to fix a pot of soup for supper. I bought a large soup bone and a bunch of other stuff I thought was appropriate and dumped it all in a big pot. I fooled with that soup two hours and it just wasn't behaving. She came in and took the lid off the pot and stirred and sniffed and said, "Ah." Then she began putting new things in and stirring and tasting and adding and that soup turned out to be first rate. Rescued soup.

She'd bring in tomatoes and onions and peppers and mushrooms and make these great sauces to go with sautéed red snapper fillets, or tuna steaks. She fixed angel hair pasta in a special way, with the red sauce pre-mixed in the pasta before it's served, and this became my favorite of all Italian dishes. She made what she called dinner pancakes, out of blue cornmeal, and stuffed with a fresh vegetable preparation.

We traveled. We ate blue corn enchiladas with green chile in Santa Fe. Hamburgers on the South Rim of the Grand Canyon. Dungeness crabs in San Francisco. Raw oysters by the dozen in New Orleans. Black beans and rice down in Key West. We ate lobster in Halifax. *Halifax.*

We went to New York and ate a wonderful meal at Le Cirque and the prices were sinful but we split the cost and did it just so I could see what it felt like. She had already done all this stuff, when I was chugging around Texas eating chicken fried steaks in places like Nacogdoches and Conroe.

This was the first woman I'd ever spent time with who had money of her own. I was used to going out with women who might have a dollar and sixty cents in a purse. This one liked to pay her own way. It didn't take me long to get used to that, especially in New York where you can pay ten bucks for a glass of wine and $32.50 for a small piece of fish on a large plate.

We'd go back and forth, from her world to mine. Sometimes I'd take her to East Texas and teach her the difference between a sweetgum and a post oak and what a rain crow sounds like and we'd eat cheese and crackers beside the road. I took her to chili cook-offs in places like Flatonia and Round Top. To a family reunion in my old hometown where we had cold barbecue sitting on the grass of the high school football field.

I showed her how to put a shiner on a fish hook and catch a bass, and she'd take the fish and make a delicious chowder. We went to baseball games where I lectured on such topics as the squeeze bunt and the infield fly rule and she asked good questions and remembered all the answers and loved the hot dogs.

We traveled, big time. We went to London and ate Dover sole and a splendid chicken pie. To the Scottish Highlands to sit up there at what seemed like the top of the world, and have salmon that wasn't three hours out of a mountain stream. We went to Paris and walked along the Seine and over the bridges and ate all the meals that are written about in books. In Austria we had the world's best breakfasts, at Salzburg, and in Venice we drank Bellinis in Harry's Bar and sat beside the Grand Canal for a meal that lasted three hours and we hated to get up and leave.

These adventures were fun and educational and expensive but they were necessary. We did all the necessary things. Then, when the time came, we stopped eating so high on the hog and began cooking heart healthy and blood pressure healthy and doing without what we really wanted. Sometimes it wasn't easy but we did without together and that made it all right.

We played tennis and golf, which I can't play but I played anyhow because she did. We pitched horseshoes. We flew kites. We got married. We shot pool. We threw a party or two. We bought a dog, and a little place in the country. We planted vegetables and flowers and put up bird houses.

Every once in a while, in honor and memory of the event that really began all this, she makes a fish chowder a lot like the one we ate out of a syrup bucket on the river that time. And when we sit down to eat at the end of the day, she doesn't mind calling it supper instead of dinner.

## Sweet Pepper and Tomato Omelettes

6-8 eggs
¼ cup milk (optional)
1 medium sweet onion
1 medium green bell pepper, seeded
½ fresh jalapeno, unpeeled, unseeded (optional)
⅔ of a 20 oz. can of San Marzano tomatoes (super-ripe
   Italian tomatoes)
1 large clove garlic
Extra virgin olive oil
A seasoned omelette pan
A separate pan for cooking filling
2 warm plates
Fresh grated parmesan cheese
Fresh ground black pepper
Salt

Dice the onion and slice the bell pepper into thin slices.
Finely chop or crush the garlic.

Heat 2 T. olive oil in a saucepan or skillet.Add the chopped
onion and pepper to the hot oil and sauté; after a few minutes,
add the chopped or crushed garlic and stir; Reduce heat to
medium.

Add the tomatoes with about ⅓ cup of their juice, breaking
the tomatoes into smaller pieces; cover and let cook for about
ten to fifteen minutes; halfway through cooking, add the
optional jalapeno, minced. (The bell peppers should be soft
and the final filling should be moist, but not juicy.) Season

with salt to taste. *If you haven't used the jalapeno, you can add a pinch of crushed red pepper here, or a few grinds of black pepper.*

*Break the eggs into a bowl. (If you want to limit your consumption of egg yolk, use eight eggs and omit four yolks.)*

*Beat the eggs lightly with a fork, adding the optional milk; season with several dashes of salt and finely ground black pepper. Set aside.*

*Heat 1 to 1½ T. olive oil in omelette pan. You want enough to film the pan on every surface the egg will touch. It's hot enough when a drop of water added to the pan sizzles and evaporates. Pour off excess.*

*Add beaten eggs, turning pan so bottom is filmed with egg. Use a spatula as the omelette cooks to lift the edges and allow more liquid egg to flow beneath the cooked part.*

*When very little liquid egg remains, place half a cup of filling—more or less, to your taste—in the center of the egg. Sprinkle with 2 T. of parmesan. Then lift the omelette pan from the heat and tilt it so the omelette slides onto one of the prepared plates. Use the edge of the pan, or a spatula to fold the last half of the omelette over the filling as it lands on the plate. (This is not as tricky as it sounds.)*

*Dust with more parmesan and freshly ground black pepper and keep warm in the oven.*

*Repeat the process with the second omelette and serve immediately.*

*Serves 2.*

## Blue Corn Dinner Pancakes with Black Beans

The recipe for the pancakes is adapted from one on the box of the mix.

> *¾ cup Blue Heaven blue corn pancake mix*
> *1 egg*
> *2½ T. olive oil*
> *¾ cup non-fat milk*
> *½ cup finely diced red onion*
> *1 medium carrot, finely diced*
> *¼ cup diced broccoli*
> *⅓ cup grated parmesan cheese*

> *(Instead of dicing by hand, we use a mini food processor.)*
> *Sauté the chopped vegetables in a little olive oil.*
> *Beat the egg lightly with the oil and milk. Stir into a bowl containing the mix.*
> *Stir in the sautéed vegetables and the cheese.*
> *Let stand five minutes.*
> *Cook on a medium-hot griddle, approximately 375 degrees.*

> *Makes 4 large pancakes.*

## Quick Black Beans

*1 can black beans*
*⅓ cup leftover spaghetti sauce*
*Ground cumin seed*
*Dried oregano*

*Rinse and drain beans. Combine in a saucepan with spaghetti sauce. Add two pinches of ground cumin and one of oregano. Heat through, stirring.*

*Serve alongside dinner pancakes.*

# Thighs in the Skillet

*6-8 chicken thighs*
*1 large carrot*
*Olive oil*
*Cayenne pepper*
*1 large onion*
*1 brown shallot*
*Tomato paste*
*Chicken broth (canned is OK)*
*1 cup vermouth*
*12 mushrooms*
*2 small garlic cloves or one large*
*Parsley*

*Trim fat from thighs. With the skin side down, season lightly with cayenne powder.*

*Heat a tablespoon of oil in an iron skillet over medium high heat. When oil is hot, tilt the pan until the bottom is filmed with oil. Take a suitable thickness of paper towel and wipe out any excess oil. Place the thighs in the hot skillet, skin side down, and brown. Adjust heat as necessary so they don't scorch.*

*Coarsely chop the onion, carrot and brown shallot. Slice the mushrooms. Chop a handful or two of parsley.*

*Turn the thighs with a spoon or tongs, taking care not to pierce. If there's more than an eighth of an inch of grease in the pan, pour it off.*

*Scatter the onion, carrot and shallot over the chicken; smear the skin side of the chicken with tomato paste.*

*Pour a cup of vermouth over everything.*

*Add the chicken broth, enough so the thighs are covered ⅔ of the way up. If you use a condensed version, you may need to thin it out with water so it isn't too salty. This is all the salt you'll need to use, so don't use unsalted broth.*

*Bring the broth to a simmer, cover the pan and cook for fifteen or so minutes.*

*Add garlic, either minced or crushed in a garlic press.*

*Add sliced mushrooms, strewing them into the liquid so they absorb its flavor.*

*Cover again and cook until done. Don't let the meat fall off the bones.*

*About ten minutes before the end, remove the lid and let the juices cook down and thicken. Sprinkle on some parsley.*

*This is delicious served with plain rice.*

*Serves 3-4.*

## Angel Hair Pasta

*1 box top quality dried angel hair pasta*
*Extra Virgin olive oil*
*1 sweet onion*
*2 large carrots, minced*
*3 large cloves of garlic*
*1 28-oz. can San Marzano tomatoes*
*1 tsp. dried oregano*
*1 bay leaf*
*Black pepper*
*Crushed red pepper*
*¾ cup pitted black Kalamara olives (brine cured, not oil*
*  cured)*
*¼ cup capers*
*2-3 anchovy fillets (optional)*
*Sugar (optional)*
*Grated fresh parmesan (optional)*

*Chop the onion coarsely and the carrot finely.*
*In a large heavy skillet over medium high heat, sauté the*
*onion and carrot in 2 T. of olive oil. Crush or finely mince the*
*garlic and add to the skillet. Cover and reduce heat to*
*medium.*
*When the onion begins to soften, add can of tomatoes with*
*their juice. Break up the pieces of tomato lightly with a fork.*
*Add oregano and bay leaf. Season with black pepper.*
*Cover and cook for ten minutes.*
*Chop olives, capers and optional anchovy. Add to the pan.*

*Cover and cook for at least twenty minutes over low heat. Taste and correct seasoning. (If onions and carrots are sweet, you won't have to add any sugar. If they aren't you may have to add a pinch or two to balance the acid in the tomatoes. Sauce should not taste sweet, but full and rich.)*

*Add a big pinch of crushed red pepper or to taste. Add salt if needed.*

*Bring 3 quarts of water to a boil.*

*Add ½ T. salt.*

*When water is boiling slide in the pasta and stir.*

*Keep a close eye on the pasta. It takes only a minute or two to cook.*

*When cooked, drain and return to pot.*

*Pour hot sauce over the pasta and return to the heat, stirring briskly to incorporate the sauce without scorching the pasta.*

*Remove from heat and serve instantly in warm bowls.*

*Add parmesan cheese if desired.*

*Serves 4*

# Guacamole Turkey Burgers

Sometimes we make this with ground buffalo meat. In that case, don't add anything but seasonings to the meat. The burgers are also good with plain ripe avocado, if you're pressed for time. The avocado or guacamole takes the place of mayonnaise.

*1 lb. ground turkey breast*
*1 slice coarse textured whole wheat bread*
*Salt*
*1 clove garlic (optional), crushed*
*Skim milk to moisten*
*Pepper*
*Olive oil*
*8 T. Marie Moore's Guacamole (See p. 160); or 1 large ripe*
    *avocado, sliced*
*2 ripe tomatoes*
*1 large sweet white or red onion*
*Red tip or leaf lettuce (you want leaves large enough to*
    *cover the meat patty)*
*12 white mushrooms*
*¼ cup red wine or sherry*
*4 whole wheat hamburger buns*
*Dijon mustard, whole grain or not, as preferred*

*Make Marie Moore's Guacamole. (See p. 160)*
*Thinly slice the onion and mushrooms.*
*Process the bread slice in a food processor to make bread*

crumbs. Add ½ tsp. salt to the crumbs and combine. Mix crumbs into the ground turkey. Add the optional garlic and a little milk to moisten. Shape into 4 patties of equal size. Season liberally with ground black pepper.

Film the bottom of a heavy skillet with olive oil and heat on medium high to high heat. Do not allow to smoke. Pour out excess oil. Add the onions to the pan, stirring, and cover. Reduce the heat.

After about five minutes, add the mushrooms and the wine.Season onions and mushrooms with salt and pepper, to taste.When onions and mushrooms are soft, remove them to a platter and keep warm.

Raise the heat and add 1 tsp. of olive oil, if necessary; when oil is hot, add the burgers. When they are seared on one side, turn them and reduce the heat to medium low. Cover the pan.

Heat the hamburger buns in the oven. Either wrap them loosely in foil for a soft bun; or toast on one side.

Wash the lettuce and slice the tomatoes; if you're not using guacamole, go ahead and peel and slice the avocado.

When the burgers are nearly done, begin assembly: Take the buns from the oven, spread the top half with 1-2 T. of guacamole; on the bottom half, spread a thin layer of Dijon mustard.

Nestle a hot burger onto the bottom half of each bun;

Place ¼ cup of sautéed onions and the same amount of sautéed mushrooms on top. (If you're using sliced avocado, instead of guacamole, you can add the slices now.) Add a lettuce leaf and a slice of ripe tomato and the top half of bun. Cut in half and serve.

Serves 4

## *Guillotine Stew*

This is Buck Sloan's name for his fish chowder, created one day at Moses Lake near Texas City "where there is a flood gate that looks like a Guillotine."

*2 lbs. potatoes, any kind*
*2 large onions*
*1 quart of tomatoes, canned or fresh (if they're ripe)*
*1 large green bell pepper*
*A man's good handful of mushrooms*
*1 quart of water*
*1 pound of shrimp, or catfish, or both*
*Seasonings, your choice: cayenne pepper or Tabasco;*
*   Worcestershire sauce; black pepper; white pepper; salt;*
*   oregano; bay leaf; garlic.*

*Peel and chop the potatoes and onions; slice the bell pepper and mushrooms;Put them in a large pot, along with the tomatoes and water and all the seasonings. Bring to a boil and cook for a little while, until the potatoes are cooked through.*
*Devein the shrimp. Skin the catfish and cut into chunks.*
*Add the shrimp and/or catfish to the pot and cook about five more minutes, until shrimp are tender and fish is done.*
*If you don't have a syrup bucket to serve it in, you can use a bowl.*

# Index